Last But Not Least

Last But Not Least

A Guide to Proofreading Text

LESLIE VERMEER

Printed and manufactured in Canada

23 24 25 26 27 5 4 3 2 1

Brush Education is located in amiskwaciwâskahikan, Edmonton, Alberta, within Treaty 6 territory and Métis Nation of Alberta Region 4, and on the traditional and ancestral territories of the Nêhiyawak, Denesuliné, Nakota Sioux, and Saulteaux Peoples.

This book is available in print, PDF, and Global Certified Acessible™ EPUB formats.

Brush Education Inc.
www.brusheducation.ca
contact@brusheducation.ca

Cover design: Dean Pickup; Cover image © Travelling-light – Dreamstime.com
Interior design and layout: Carol Dragich, Dragich Design
Proofreading: Mary Lou Roy

Image credits: 5.1: Igor Kyrlysta, ShutterStock vector ID 1025539069; Oleksandr Yuhlichek, ShutterStock vector ID 1025539069. 6.2a: iStock.com/urbazon. 6.2b: iStock.com/michaeljung. 6.3c: iStock.com/ingenui. 7.1 top: B. Timothy Keith; markup text used by permission of NeWest Press. 7.1 bottom: Colby Clair Stolson; markup text used by permission of Brush Education Inc. Author photo courtesy of MacEwan University.

Library and Archives Canada Cataloguing in Publication

Title: Last but not least : a guide to proofreading text / Leslie Vermeer.

Names: Vermeer, Leslie, 1969- author.

Description: Includes bibliographical references and index.

Identifiers: Canadiana (print) 20190164808 | Canadiana (ebook) 20190164840 | ISBN 9781550597875 (softcover) | ISBN 9781550597882 (PDF) | ISBN 9781550597905 (EPUB)

Subjects: LCSH: Proofreading. | LCSH: Proofreading—Problems, exercises, etc.

Classification: LCC Z254 .V47 2021 | DDC 808.02/7—dc23

We acknowledge the support of the Government of Canada
Nous reconnaissons l'appui du gouvernement du Canada | Canadä

For Garry. Here's to the days
when we could solve
the problems of the world over coffee.

Contents

Acknowledgements

For an editor, writing a book about proofreading is an undertaking that weds chutzpah and high anxiety. I am grateful to have had such tremendous support in this project. My thanks to Glenn Rollans for his enthusiasm about the book; to Lauri Seidlitz for her generous, insightful editing and her meticulous care for words and ideas; to Kay Rollans for her gentle but firm cheerleading; to Carol Dragich for her clear and thoughtful design; and to the entire team at Brush Education for their patience and encouragement.

I would like to acknowledge and thank the editors and writers who lent their expertise to the tips and advice in chapter 7: Norma Jean Brown, Carmen Hrynchuk, Claire Kelly, Anne Nothof, Garry Ryan, and Earl J. Woods. Thanks also to Belinda Panganiban for her insights into transcription and her encouragement. Extra-special thanks to Bruce Keith for his help with design and production content.

Finally, I'd like to extend a big thank you to my editing students over the years for their questions about and insights into proofreading. Their engagement has pushed and challenged my thinking and teaching.

The exercise "Spelling Test" on page 91 is inspired by an exercise in *Correct Writing*, 6th edition, by Butler et al. (1995).

The exercise "Breaking Context" on page 93 is inspired by an outstanding exercise in Kay Vanstone's book *Practical Proofreading*, 2nd edition (1997).

Introduction

Proofreading refers to a close read-through to confirm that the text of a document — whether on paper, on a screen, or in another format — will appear as intended. Proofreading is not the kind of reading we do every day — in fact, it's not really "reading" at all. Rather, it involves examining words letter by letter, then assembling those letters and words into units of meaning.

p / r / o / o / f / r / e / a / d / n / g

If you read the line above closely, rather than assuming from context what it said, then you noticed the missing character. Congratulations! You're on your way.

Who is this book for?

This book has been written for anyone who works with words and is responsible for their accuracy and consistency. You might be an administrative assistant responsible for creating and distributing letters, memos, and reports on behalf of others. You might be a communications staffer responsible for generating social media updates, blog posts, brochures, or sell copy. You might be a technical writer who must ensure readers are not distracted by misspellings or missed words as they work through complex processes or procedures. You might be a teacher, a researcher, or a paralegal — or maybe even a student looking to improve your academic achievement by catching the little errors that mask your true ability. Whoever you are, wherever you work,

you *can* learn to improve the quality of the documents you produce. The techniques and procedures in this book will teach you how to proofread your way to excellent documents.

Readers react to the quality of the text they read, even when they can't clearly articulate what's wrong with the text. Readers trust clean, well-written prose more than they trust misspelled or badly punctuated messages. While there are many places where we can let down our language defences (e.g., in text messages), in almost every professional setting, our credibility and competence are judged by the correctness, consistency, and clarity of our writing. Proofreading, then, is an important way to signal care, commitment to quality, and overall professionalism. This is the service that you, as proofreader, provide.

Proofreading is a valuable, portable skill that is needed in almost every field and industry. Your ability to spot errors and to correct them before they become permanent and public will make you immensely valuable to colleagues, employers, and clients.

What is proofreading?

While most of us notice some proofreading errors in the reading we do from day to day, the process of proofreading is distinct from ordinary reading. Proofreading is a specific process of reviewing communication in the context of a particular document. In a professional publishing setting, proofreading is the final stage before a document is published but after it is formatted (for print or screen).

The job of the proofreader is to remove any last mistakes or blemishes that have not been caught during earlier reviews and edits. The work is done one word at a time, one line at a time, with a clear awareness of typical weak spots in communication. A proofreader checks for several kinds of concerns — spelling, punctuation, grammar, sense and accuracy, visual presentation, and overall consistency — and works at a depth or level appropriate for the situation. Most importantly, the proofreader holds a specific mindset: anticipating errors but respecting earlier processes and decision making.

This kind of work requires discipline and focus. You must approach the document slowly, calmly, and methodically. Proofreading is challenging because it demands that you slow down. Most of us, because we work under immense time pressure, tend to want to work faster, not slow down. But there's no way around it. Effective proofreading requires concentration. You can't give a document your full attention when you're rushing.

What isn't proofreading?

One of the most difficult ideas to grasp about proofreading is that it is both meticulous and superficial. It is meticulous in the sense that it is highly detailed; but it is superficial because you are not rewriting or re-editing the text in front of you. While you must expect to find errors, you must also assume that most of the text is very close to final.

Proofreading isn't copyediting. If you're rewriting phrases and sentences, adding or deleting content, or reorganizing the structure and flow of a document, you're not proofreading: you're working too deep. If you're making big changes on your document, finish your work at that depth and then proofread the document later. Proofreading involves polishing the surface of a well-made document to ensure it's as close to perfect as possible.

About this book

This book assumes you are someone who works with words — an office staffer, a social media specialist, or an editor, for instance. For that reason, the exercises and activities are written to reflect a variety of professional and organizational settings. But these skills are just as relevant for undergraduate and graduate students, particularly because academic integrity and honour codes insist that students do their own work and not rely on others to edit and proofread for them except under specific circumstances.

Further, this book assumes that you have a fairly confident grasp of grammar and punctuation. A book about proofreading must, obviously, deal primarily with the skills of proofreading and cannot include extensive discussions of grammar, punctuation, mechanics, or related areas. (There are numerous books that *do* cover those topics in depth, however — see appendix 5 for some titles.) If your knowledge or skills feel a little rusty, you can take advantage of the punctuation and grammar primers in appendices 1 and 2. If not, you can jump confidently into chapter 1. You'll also find a glossary at the back of the book to define various terms and concepts, highlighted throughout the book in SMALL CAPS.

Chapter 1 forms the foundation of the book. It provides specific instruction about how, when, and why we proofread, from where proofreading fits in the production sequence of documents to how to make proofreading marks. Chapters 2 to 6 are each organized

> **Proofreading involves polishing the surface of a well-made document to ensure it's as close to perfect as possible.**

PROOFREADING VERSUS COPYEDITING

Look at the following short paragraph. The first markup reflects how a copyeditor might treat the text. The second markup reflects how a proofreader might treat the same text. What an editor does, of course, varies with the editor's authority and the text's context, but the contrast in these treatments should give you a general sense of the distinction between proofreading and copyediting.

(copyediting)

Peaceful and cool, pastel ~~shades of~~ green lend a calming note in the bathroom or bedroom. Darker greens, on the other hand, are best reserved for accents. ~~We identify~~ *are often identified* these colours with leaves, grass, and water, so ~~don't be afraid to~~ *you can* amplify a natural theme with organic shapes and textures.

(proofreading)

Peaceful and cool, pastel shades of green lend a calming note in the bathroom or bedroom. Darker greens, on the other hand, are best reserved for accents. We identify these colours with leaves, grass, and water, so don't be afraid to amplify a natural theme with organic shapes and textures.

---

around a specific focus: spelling, grammar, or production, for instance. Chapter 7 brings our topic to a conclusion with a selection of further tips and tricks and the introduction of what I call the proofreading state of mind. Each chapter opens with a quick warm-up exercise to get you thinking about the kinds of things to look for as a proofreader. In every chapter you'll also find exercises keyed to specific skills as well as tips aimed at helping you develop a careful, thorough proofreading process that you can bring to any text. Chapter 8 contains additional exercises, which can be used for standalone practice or in conjunction with chapters 1 through 7. And in the back matter you'll find additional resources to help your skills and knowledge grow.

This book refers to both on-paper and onscreen work. Perhaps paper seems irrelevant in our highly digital world, but ink continues to be applied to paper (and other SUBSTRATES) in many, many settings. For the purpose of learning about proofreading, it's not the medium that matters. What matters is your proofreading mindset: being prepared to find errors and knowing how to resolve them.

The main text of this book uses Canadian spelling and largely follows *The Chicago Manual of Style*, 17th edition (henceforth the *Chicago Manual*). The exercises and examples also use Canadian spelling as a default, but other mechanical styling varies. For example, some exercises use the serial comma; others don't. Proofreading demands that you notice patterns in text (such as the presence or absence of serial commas) and respond appropriately in context (by following the direction of the assigned style guide, for example).

In several of the exercises, I have suggested that you query any issues other than those at the heart of the exercise (such as spelling). You might, for example, query a turn of phrase that seems clichéd, or strange to your ear. Or you might query a fact that doesn't seem factual to you. I cannot anticipate everything you might query, so in most cases I haven't included queries in the answer keys.

If you do write a query for an exercise, you might want to discuss it with someone, such as a teacher or a colleague. The conversation could prove valuable to your growth as a proofreader. But remember that proofreaders are generally restricted by their role: they correct outright errors but query anything else. So although you might not like the voice and phrasing in a document, unless it is patently incorrect or inconsistent with the larger purpose of that document, as a proofreader, you let it stand. This is one of the toughest points of discipline in proofreading — but it's vital to the proofreader's efficiency and dexterity.

Proofreading happens late in the process of document production, but it's crucial that you resist the temptation to hurry. The title of this book, *Last But Not Least*, should be an important touchstone for your approach to the vital and valuable work of proofreading.

1

How to Proofread

The Basics

Compare the nonsense character strings below. Can you spot the differences?
Answers on page 19.

1. a. oilylilylillyoil   b. oilyliiylillyoil   c. oilylilylillyoil

2. a. 8&%8%&8&§¢8999   b. 8&%8%&3&§¢8999   c. 8&%8%&8&§¢9999

3. a. idkjkidkjkidkkk   b. idkjkidkjkidkkk   c. idkjkidkjkibkkk

4. a. ?!?!?!?#####!?!?!##   b. ?!?!?!?####!?!?!##   c. ?!?!?!?####!?!?!##

5. a. mnrmmmmmnrnnnmnrrrr   b. mmrmmmmmnrnnnmnrrrr   c. mnrmmmmmnrnnnmnnrrr

6. a. 55S555SS55S555SSS55S   b. 55S555SS55S555SSS55S   c. 55S555SS55S555SSS5SS

In its *Professional Editorial Standards* (2016), Editors Canada defines proofreading as the process of "examining material after layout or in its final format to correct errors in textual and visual elements." What this definition means is that a proofreader is responsible for checking every part of every page and ensuring the document communicates correctly and effectively. The proofreader's job is to correct misspellings, find any faulty grammar and MECHANICS, ensure consistency and correctness, note or correct deviations from visual specifications, and catch any other glaring errors. Unless the proofreader has been given explicit permission to work deeper, she queries anything else. The proofreader is not the author and is not the copyeditor; she is a backup for both.

Of course, you may have written the document yourself, and/or you may have copyedited the document. For our purposes here, though, regardless of the work you may already have done on the document, I assume you are proofreading as a distinct step in producing your document. This assumption applies regardless of what kind of documents you produce and the speed with which you produce them. Without some distance — intellectual or temporal — from the text, your proofreading is likely to be ineffective.

The ground rules

Let's start with some basic assumptions. For the purposes of our discussion, there are four distinct steps between a writer's intention to write and the audience's reception of the writing.

1. Creation — to the point of a stable final or near-final draft
2. Editing — undertaken by the writer or someone else, or by the writer in collaboration with someone else
3. Formatting — sometimes a lengthy and complex step, but sometimes minimal
4. Proofreading

Because proofreading happens last in this process, a proofreader must assume that the document is final except for tiny last-minute changes. The document is no longer at a stage for rewriting or recasting. If something requires rewriting or recasting, you must do that work and then start proofreading again.

With these thoughts in mind, here are the ground rules for successful proofreading:

1. The process requires time, space, and distance.
2. Correct only mistakes; query all other issues.
3. Respect your boundaries. You are not the author or the copyeditor. (Well, okay, perhaps you are, but even so, you need to push yourself out of these roles for the sake of the process.)

I recognize that sometimes circumstances overtake proofreaders and we have to compromise. Throughout the book you'll find tips for triaging text when your time is sharply limited. By EDITORIAL TRIAGE I mean you must assess how urgent textual issues are and determine your top priorities. Then you can decide how you will treat them, in what order, and with what methods.

WHAT IS COPYEDITING?

This is a book dedicated to proofreading, but from time to time I refer to an earlier editing stage called *copyediting*. Although proofreading and copyediting are in many ways complementary skills, copyediting involves working much deeper in a document than proofreading does. Copyeditors deal with issues of coherence, clarity, correctness, and consistency, applying an enormous range of decisions to suit the audience and the purpose of the communication. Copyediting may also involve fact checking and rewriting. Proofreading is much more cosmetic by comparison, but no less important: it's the final polish to ensure no errors remain in the text or its formatting.

As you evaluate whether to make a change, when it's not obvious whether you should do so or not, here are two questions to ask yourself:

1. What's best for the intended audience? (That is, will making this change make the document better for its readers?)
2. What's easiest for the process at this stage? (That is, do you risk introducing a further error or holding up publication?)

These questions won't tell you what to do, but they will narrow your perspective on the problem. The easiest solution isn't always the best solution, nor are readers the only consideration when you're making changes; but when you're under pressure to make a decision quickly, having a tight focus can help.

Proofreading is an editing step, but it is not a lighter form of copyediting: it is a distinct process. Sometimes your proofreading work on a document will look like a light copyedit (especially if you're the first person other than the writer to review the document). That's okay! Keep going at that depth, and recognize that you (or another person) will need to

THE PUBLISHING SEQUENCE

Traditional print publication follows a specific, logical sequence. Digital communication and informal publication will often follow the same steps, but there may also be differences.

1. **Creation**: A writer (or a group of contributors) creates a document.

2. **Substantive review**: The creator, often in conjunction with an editor, multiple editors, or other experts, examines the content and structure of the document closely. The content and structure are refined to suit the intended audience and the expected purpose of the document.

3. **Copyedit**: The document is edited for style, correctness, and consistency. If fact checking is part of the process, it occurs now. A particular mechanical style (e.g., Canadian Press style, APA style) may be applied at this stage.

4. **Formatting**: This step may involve formal design and layout work or, in some environments (such as working on a blog), it may involve applying preset styles (e.g., heading levels, alignment, italics) and adding visual content.

5. **Proofreading**: Here at last is the step this book is interested in! The document is almost ready to meet its readership. We proofread to ensure the text and its visual presentation are as close to perfect — and as close to its creator's intentions — as possible. (In some workflows, the written text is proofread before formatting. Another proofread must be done after formatting to confirm the text is complete and has been correctly placed and to review the visual elements of the document.)

6. **Publication**: The document becomes available to readers (sometimes after additional production and duplication steps).

Obviously, in some communication situations (e.g., a social media update), these steps are greatly compressed and occur rapidly (and yes, you should proofread your social media posts with the same mindset you adopt for other documents). In other situations, these steps may involve months or even years of work.

proofread the document again — to confirm that the document is correct and consistent after all the changes you have introduced.

The proofreader upholds the deliberate choices made at earlier stages in document creation; these could be entirely conventional or radically experimental. It's your job to ensure that what is captured in the document is what is intended to reach public eyes. Never assume that an editing decision was careless or thoughtless. If you are working with a copyeditor who has gone through the document before you receive it, you may have received a STYLE SHEET listing deliberate choices and styles to be applied to the document. You may

Your job is to catch any remaining errors, not to judge the choices made at an earlier stage of document production.

also be working with an assigned style guide (sometimes called a style manual) or a local style sheet, as we'll discuss later. It's important not to overrule the earlier editor's decisions, even if your tastes and preferences differ. You risk introducing errors and inconsistencies if you do so. Remember, your job is to catch any remaining errors, not to judge the choices made at an earlier stage of document production.

The document a proofreader works on is normally *composed*, or laid out; that is, it appears in the visual format that its eventual reader will see. That might be a document formatted with layout software such as Adobe InDesign, or prepared in a blogging tool like WordPress, but it might also be a document created in Microsoft Word that's about to be sent to its intended recipient. For the proofreader, visual elements are as important as textual elements, and both require scrutiny.

Thus, while proofreading may be the last time a writer or editor reviews the text, this step is very important — last, but definitely not least!

Boundaries

When you proofread, you face some real limitations. First, you need to know or identify the existing style of the document and your level of authority to overrule what exists on the page. Second, you need to consider the amount of time available to complete the task and how missing a deadline will affect processes down the line. Finally, you need to evaluate the work in its context. How short-lived or enduring will this document be? What are the expectations of its readers? What are the consequences of failing to meet those expectations?

Authority is serious. As proofreader, you have only so much latitude to make changes. Other people involved in earlier processes may have a longer view of the project; they know why certain decisions have been made and why certain steps cannot be taken. It's your job to bring the text *as it stands* as close to perfect as possible, not to fix the text to your tastes.

Time, as the saying goes, is always of the essence. Proofreading happens late in the process of creating a document for circulation or publication, whether that means clicking *publish* on blogging software, sealing a signed letter in an envelope, or sending a file to be manufactured into thousands of copies of a book. There's lots of pressure to hurry. Sometimes meeting your time limits means you can concentrate on only essential errors; sometimes it means parcelling out the work to others and coordinating their CATCHES (the errors a proofreader has found). Always estimate generously how much time you're going to need to complete your work. A practised proofreader can work through about 250 words in 6 or 7 minutes, not including time for cross-checking references or consulting resources. If your documents are complex, budget extra time — and remember that you should plan to go through the entire document *at least* twice. (More about this point later.)

Time is often related to money. Few organizations can afford to invest large sums in proofreading, yet organizations also want to uphold their reputations through high-quality communication. Many people work in settings where a moment's inattention can have high costs, financial or otherwise. Part of managing time well may involve teaching others in your environment to respect the time proofreading requires.

The best proofreaders find every error within their authority and don't waste time or money with unnecessary questions. That said, they also know how to distribute their efforts over, say, a promotional flyer versus an annual report. You will find yourself weighing competing demands: the rigour of the task versus the time available, or the resources available

> **It's your job to bring the text *as it stands* as close to perfect as possible, not to fix the text to your tastes.**

AUTHORITY AND RESPONSIBILITY

For many people, the idea of editorial triage bumps uncomfortably against the goal of getting things perfectly right. The thing about that goal is that communication isn't perfect: it's a set of conventions that humans have more or less agreed to follow. What's "perfect" to me might not be "perfect" to you, even if we both consult external authorities to validate our perspectives. Proofreading is about making text correct, not perfect.

Just the same, there are times when a proofreader receives text that is objectively subpar. You know it when you see it: dense, jargon-filled academic writing that doesn't make sense; corporate reports laden with business clichés and bloviation; overdone documents from novice communicators trying to effect the sound of gravitas. Where do you start proofreading a document that is grammatically sound but not well written or appealing? That is, which errors or issues must you change and which do you live with? You must recognize and apply your boundaries.

A scale for evaluating your choices

Here is a rough scale for triaging textual problems. Depending on your situation, you may have other factors to evaluate, too, including time, costs, and the roles of other people.

- Is the issue simply a typo? If yes, fix it.
- Is the issue grammatically incorrect? If yes, fix it.
- Is the issue potentially dangerous for the writer, the publisher, or the reader? If yes, fix it.
- Is the issue potentially embarrassing for the writer or the publisher? If yes, fix it.
- Is a fact obviously wrong? If yes, fix it or query it.
- Is the issue inconsistent with choices made elsewhere in the document? If yes, fix it or query it.
- Is the issue stylistically inappropriate for the intended audience (e.g., slang in formal writing, jargon in informal writing)? Does its presence draw attention away from the document's content? If yes, fix it or query it.
- Is the issue a matter of correct but poor phrasing? If yes, query it or leave it alone.
- Is the issue an awkward or confusing idea or explanation? If yes, query it or leave it alone.
- Will resolving the issue require multiple changes? If yes, query it or leave it alone.
- Is the issue something most ordinary readers would notice? If no, leave it alone. If yes, fix it or query it.
- Will the reader benefit from the time invested in solving the problem? If no, leave it alone. If yes, fix it or query it.

You might also need to consider who edited the document before you received it and where the document will go next.

Continued on page 6.

My intention with this scale is to help you focus tightly on the task of proofreading and to move away from the ideal of perfection. Proofreading is not about our personal language tastes; it's about creating effective communication. Which choices will be most effective for the document's intended reader? Which choices make little or no difference to anyone but other editors? Remember, *it is not a failure to recognize that sometimes the best a text can be is correct and not good.*

versus the potential consequences of an error. Correctness always matters, but when time is pinched, consistency might be sacrificed.

The reality is that you might be the writer, the editor, and now the proofreader. In this case, time is your top priority: you need enough time to gain distance from the document. Without sufficient time, you may struggle to perceive what the text actually says. If you can, get a colleague to bring fresh eyes to the text, and give yourself as much time away from the document as possible so when you do look at it, you can spot any lingering errors as if they were someone else's. As technical editor Michael Alley observes, "Proofreading is not a glory task — it is a responsibility task." With that idea in mind, let's look at what to do and how to do it.

Proofreading method and process

As a basic method, plan to work through the document at three levels, or in three ways. Each level may require multiple passes (a PASS in this sense means a complete read-through of the text).

1. **The preparatory level**: This is a planning or previewing pass, when you evaluate the degree of work likely to be needed. Identify any obvious problems or concerns and note any areas that will require extra attention. Skipping this step could lead to nasty surprises (if you encounter things in the text for which you're not prepared) and can cause delays later in the process. Gather the resources you will need, find a quiet,

well-lit location, and block out ample time to do the work.

2. **The sustained level**: Slowly read through the document as a continuous text, carefully proofreading letter by letter, word by word. Examine spelling, punctuation, grammar, usage, meaning, accuracy, and visual presentation. You will likely make repeated passes at this level, focussing on different elements each time, such as running heads and footers, cross-references to the notes and bibliography, and captions. Expect to work through the document at least twice. Make the changes you've caught so far; then start with an unmarked-up version and concentrate on reading like elements together. For example, read all the section opening pages together to compare their formatting, or read all the exercises in sequence to confirm they're correctly numbered and placed, with no repetition. Mark any further changes and confirm that all catches have been corrected and no new errors have been introduced (see chapter 7). Note: if you are still making a substantial number of changes at this point, or if multiple proofreaders are working on the document, plan at least one more complete read-through at this level (and possibly more), ideally with some time away from the document or by someone who has not proofread it before. This extra pass helps you ensure correctness, consistency, and coherence after extensive intervention.

3. **The snapshot level**: When you're fairly confident the document is clean, go through it completely one more time. Relax and let your eyes roam around the text at random. Sometimes an error will pop out at a glance, even though you haven't seen it before. If time permits and fresh eyes are available, have someone else look at the document in the same relaxed manner. Make any final changes, and the document should be ready to go. (If you work in a traditional publishing workflow, a few days or weeks later there may be yet another set of proofs, these usually with restrictive deadlines and high costs for last-minute changes. Make only essential changes then.)

The idea of making multiple passes through a document is a big sticking point for many proofreaders. If you're good, you shouldn't need multiple passes, right? Wrong. Multiple passes are not a waste of time or a sign of weakness; they're a mark of a thorough process. Don't assume you can bring equal focus to every part of the document when you look at the whole thing at once: you can't. Instead, concentrate element by element until you run out of time or you're confident you've found as much as you can. Then let the document go.

It's a truism in conventional publishing that a book must be proofread by at least three sets of eyes. That's not a bad idea. Every proofreader has a different sensibility and responds to different issues. Particularly if the stakes for a document are high, use multiple proofreaders (including the writer, if available, and at least one person who is unfamiliar with the text), and lean on digital tools carefully for extra support. A slow, conscientious process is efficient if people are following the ground rules I laid out above, and lends an extra level of confidence. (If accuracy is paramount, hiring a professional external proofreader in such situations is not an admission of weakness or defeat. It is an acknowledgement that proofreading is difficult work and that some jobs require intense scrutiny.)

You also have an excellent learning opportunity when you work with multiple proofreaders, including external professionals. When you are CONSOLIDATING CHANGES, observe each proofreader's strengths and weaknesses — including your own. Then follow up by looking for opportunities to teach and learn from one another, so you and the people you work with can grow stronger together. Also remember that while most queries will go back to the document's editor for review and decision, it's a good idea to share proofreading changes and queries with the writer, too — writers also learn from the process.

QUERIES

Different proofreaders handle queries in different ways. At this stage, if all has gone well with earlier stages of editing, you shouldn't expect to generate many queries. If you're working on paper, keep a running list of queries on a piece of paper or a digital file, or write queries on the document itself (on the RECTO in the margin or on the VERSO so that queries are separate from the markup). Clearly indicate where the query occurs, either with a circled question mark or the circled letters QU in the margin. Numbering your queries on the manuscript can make referring back to your running list easier, but can become unwieldy if you're working on a long project; in that case, simply use page numbers. If your workflow is entirely digital, record your queries using the comment function in Adobe Acrobat or Microsoft Word; the software itself sequences your queries for later review.

Version management

When a process involves multiple proofreaders, one person's job is to collect all the catches and transfer them to a single document (and resolve any queries). In a traditional

QUERIES: HOW TO ASK GOOD QUESTIONS

Queries are questions about the text that the proofreader cannot answer by herself. At this stage, queries should be brief and clear; the respondent should be able to answer "yes," "no," or "doesn't matter" to most of them. Here are some examples of good proofreading queries:

- *Does this quotation require a page citation?*
- *"Intrapsychic" is spelled closed (with no space or hyphen) four times and as "intra-psychic" four times. Should all instances be closed?*
- *Does "this" refer to the situation or our understanding of the situation? Insert a noun after "this" to clarify?*
- *Are you referring to the restaurant Woods on Highway 40? Note no apostrophe.*

One of the fundamentals of writing good queries is remembering your role and your boundaries. Don't query points you should reasonably be expected to know, particularly at this stage of document production. For instance, don't query how to spell a word correctly (unless it is highly unusual or there is an issue with consistency); just mark it up spelled correctly. Also, don't query something just because you don't like the writer's point of view or disagree with the writer's premise or conclusion — that's beyond your scope. Here's a smart guideline: *query only what the intended audience would likely query.*

publishing workflow, this is the responsibility of the project editor or assigning editor. At this stage of document production, version management is crucial, so *only one* person should control the most-current version of the document and make changes. Otherwise, you risk making changes to an outdated version of the document, overwriting someone else's changes, wasting your own and your colleagues' time, and leaving errors in place in the most current version.

Similarly, when you are working with material available in multiple formats, there must be one master document and one person responsible for it. A change in one format (prior to publication) must echo through all subsequent versions, and any late corrections on one version need to be captured on the master document and documents derived from it. Particularly in distributed workflows, it's important that any proofreading changes be communicated to the person responsible for custody of the master document.

Style sheets help you succeed

A STYLE SHEET is a project-specific record of decisions a writer or editor compiles as she or he works through a document (see figure 1.1 for an example). It may be supported by a style guide such as *The Canadian Press Stylebook* or *MLA Handbook for Writers of Research Papers*. The purpose of a style sheet is consistency. It captures decisions such as the handling of the SERIAL COMMA, how numbers are treated, how dates are formatted, and which spellings have been changed to conform to the project dictionary (or which spellings should *not* change). It may also include unusual spelling or usage decisions, proper names with unusual features, and abbreviations or acronyms specific to the project or the organization.

When you receive a document to proofread, you may receive a style sheet to go with it. As you complete the proofreading, add any new style points you apply. These additions may be helpful to the person making changes to the master document and may form the

STYLE SHEET: LOIS ALWAYS LED WITH A STORY

— spelling follows *Canadian Oxford Dictionary*, 2nd ed.
— inline citations, bibliography follow MLA
— publication styling follows *Chicago Manual of Style*, 17th ed.

Mechanics

series comma in
dashes set wide
numbers are spelled out
    (except where cumbersome), including
    even hundreds, even thousands
heights: six foot four, a six-foot-tall man
no period after chapter number in ToC
LC after colon
grades: spelled out, LC
no hyphen in -ly compounds
    (e.g., culturally appropriate)

Spelling, Usage

9/11
A-okay
adrenalin (no final E)
after-grad party
baba ghanouj
backdate (closed)
backyard (closed)
barrelling, barrelled (doubled L)
bed-head
blowout (N)
box spring (open)
break-up (N)
camp-out
cell phone (open)
chain-link fence
chinook (no capital)
cinderbrick (closed)
clean-up (N), clean-out (N)
co-operation, co-operative
coexist, coexistence
combover (N)
cooties

councillor (re municipal leadership)
crow-hop (N and V)
deadbolt (closed)
drive-by, drive-bys
enrolment (single L)
face down
fast-forward
favour
firefighter
focussed, focussing
free-for-all (N)
french fries (note no capital)
fuelling, fuelled (doubled L)
goodbye (closed)
grey (not gray)
grow-op
hairspray
half-sister (hyphen, not open)
hard-ass (N)
haymow
head gate
hiccup
high-rise (N)
hungover (ADJ)
judgement
levelled (doubled L)
light bulb (open)
manoeuvre (N and V)
Ms. (note period)
nonfiction (closed, not non-fiction)
nonverbal (no hyphen)
okay (not OK)
paycheque
percent (closed, not per cent)
pickup (truck)
Powwow

(continued on next page)

Figure 1.1 There are many ways to make a style sheet; pay attention to what is captured on this one. This sample was compiled by a copyeditor and would be supplied to the proofreader. The editor uses several initialisms: ToC for "table of contents," LC for "lower case," N for "noun," and ADJ for "adjective."

practice (N), practise (V)	Sweat Lodge
pre-emptive (hyphenated)	time frame (open, no hyphen)
rear-view mirror	timeout (N)
seafoam green	toque
seat belt (open)	toward (not towards)
shovelling (doubled L)	travelling
show-and-tell	trick-or-treating
side arms	TV (not T.V.)
sidesaddle (closed)	underway (closed)
sidetracked	US (not U.S.)
smartass (N)	vice-principal
sound check	videotape, videotaping
soundguy	walk-through (N)
steampunk (closed)	white-tailed deer
storey, storeys	wide-mouth Mason jar
storytelling	World War II (not Two)
sucker-punch	X-ray (note capital)

Figure 1.1 continued.

basis of style decisions for future projects. The example style sheet in figure 1.1 should give you a sense of what to expect.

In some workflows, you may be able to support your proofreading process with language tools such as Grammarly or PerfectIt, which find spelling errors, inconsistencies, and some kinds of composition errors. If you use such tools, note any style-related changes you accept on the style sheet in case you need to change them back. (Always remember that these tools can find only some issues; they are not a substitute for thorough proofreading.)

On some projects you will have to create the style sheet as you go. Start by writing down the dictionary and style guide assigned to the project, if any. (If nothing has been specified, you should choose appropriate resources yourself, so you must know the audience and purpose for the document.) Local decisions, sometimes called *house style*, may overrule the dictionary or style guide, so be alert to any apparently deliberate exceptions (you

may need to query these points). Then write down anything you encounter that requires changing to make it consistent (don't record the outright errors you've caught and corrected). Record proper names as you encounter them, along with the context of their first instance (e.g., the page number), so that you can control consistency across the span of the document (e.g., *Vicki* versus *Victoria* or *Toyah Willcox* versus *Toyah Ann Willcox*). If the style guide or dictionary gives you a choice about treatment, write down your decision. Don't try to hold everything in your memory. At this stage your style sheet shouldn't be very long.

A style sheet is a tool to help you work efficiently. If writers you work with have particular foibles, record the consistent solution on a personal style sheet and keep it handy when you collaborate. Similarly, if there's a style rule or a spelling you have trouble remembering, write it on your personal style sheet instead of looking it up every time. The reinforcement of seeing this information regularly will help you retain it; good discipline makes your work easier and more confident.

One point that can be difficult for proofreaders occurs when we encounter decisions we don't agree with. For example, many editors prefer to use the serial comma, but it is omitted in most journalistic writing as a matter of style, and a proofreader doesn't have the authority to overrule this convention. If you notice a point of style that you dislike but that is not actually wrong and has been made consistently, *don't change it*. Trying to override a consistent choice means you risk introducing inconsistency and errors into the document at a very late stage — exactly the opposite of what proofreading is meant to accomplish.

The style sheet, alongside the project dictionary and the style guide, is central to proofreading. Your role is to apply conformity to decisions made earlier and to ensure the correctness of various aspects of the document. The style may not be one you like, but it's your job to apply it correctly and consistently.

Making and reading markup symbols

The concept behind using markup symbols is brevity. Because proofreading happens late in the process, proofreaders don't have time to write out complex instructions. The symbols function as shorthand, taking the place of lengthy explanations. Even if your workflow is strictly digital, you should know the basic markup symbols. Tools like Adobe Acrobat Pro use them, and the symbols can save time if everyone in your workflow understands them. See pages 12 and 13 for examples of markup symbols and their use.

Proofreading symbols are used with the assumption that the publication process is almost finished, so they are direct (for brevity) and compact (to save space). You *double mark* the text when you proofread — that is, you place a caret (an insertion mark) or a dele (a deletion mark) in the line, then mark the change or correction in the margin beside the line. You can use either margin, but many proofreaders prefer the right-hand margin, both for consistency and because English reads left to right. Note that words and phrases to be inserted are not written in the inter-line space because there usually isn't enough room to write them neatly. If a line or more must be changed, cross it out and write the replacement text neatly in the margin (or on a separate sheet if the passage is lengthy; if you're working onscreen, you can key in the replacement text to be cut, formatted, and pasted in). The sample markups in figures 1.2a and b should give you a sense of what to do.

Of course, all this instruction assumes your colleagues and clients understand markup symbols, too. If you think the person receiving the markup and making the changes may not understand your symbols, then change your tactics to accommodate the situation. Be tidy and be consistent: these two qualities help tremendously. Also take time to explain your markup so your work isn't misunderstood or incompletely incorporated. Even if the person does understand markup symbols, ensure that what you want is unambiguously indicated. The person making the changes may be rushed or worrying about other elements of the document. Your clarity helps reduce errors and ensures that critical corrections will be adopted. If the person making changes doesn't understand your markup, he or she may make an error that results in more passes and more changes. Every change at the end stage carries with it the potential for error.

You may think it's not necessary to learn proofreading symbols today, but the symbols are common to many disciplines in both print and digital, visual and textual forms. Although proofreading conventions arose in the days of metal type, the communicative efficiency of the symbols remains unsurpassed.

STANDARD MARKUP SYMBOLS

Delete a letter	This sentence contains an extra letter.
Delete a word	This sentence contains an extra ~~extra~~ word.
Insert a character	This sentence is mising a letter. /s
Insert a word	A word is from this sentence. / missing
Change a letter	The vowel in the word blew needs to be changed. /o
Change a word	A word in this sentence needs to be ~~changed~~. / corrected
Close up unwanted space	This sentence shows the preferred spelling of super/hero. ⊂
Delete unwanted space	This sentence contains an /unwanted space. / ⌣
Insert space	This sentence needs aspace inserted. / #
Transpose letters	This sentence uses dairy as an example. (tr)
Transpose a word or phrase	This sentence contains in the wrong order words and phrases. (tr)
Move to the left	This sentence needs to be pushed left.
Move to the right	This sentence needs to be pushed right.
Centre align	This sentence should be centred in its column.
Move up	This sentence should appear higher on the page.
Move down	This sentence should appear lower on the page.
Make a letter upper case	this sentence should start with a capital letter. (cap)
Make a letter lower case	This Sentence doesn't Require so many Capital letters. (lc)
Set a word all upper case	This sentence includes a phrase to set in all caps. (caps)
Make a series of letters lower case	This sentence doesn't require ~~ALL CAPS.~~ (lc)
Set italic	We use italics on words used as terms and on some foreign words. (ital)
Set ROMAN	Roman text is normal typography without bold or italics. *This sentence has been wrongly set in italics.* (rom)
Set boldface	We use boldface to make text stand out. (bf)

Set in small caps	We can also use small caps for emphasis. (sc)
Correct typeface	Part of this sentence has been intentionally set in the wrong font. (wf)
Make a character superscript	This sentence shows you how to mark 10⁹. (super)
Make a character subscript	This sentence shows you how to mark CO2. (sub)
Insert a period	This sentence should end with a period. / ⊙
Insert a comma	There should be a comma in this sentence please. / ⌃
Insert an apostrophe	We mustnt omit the apostrophe in this sentence. / ⌄
Insert a question mark	Do you know how to mark up a sentence as a question. / ?
Insert quotation marks	The writer said, Use quotation marks around direct speech. / ⌄ / ⌄
Insert a hyphen	This sentence should include a well loved hyphen. / =
Insert an en dash	This sentence includes an en dash to indicate a date range (1984 1986). / ¹/N
Insert an em dash	In this sentence, the use of an em dash the punctuation dash indicates interruption. / ¹/M / ¹/M
Insert parentheses	Parentheses in this sentence enclose asides and other less important information. / (/)
Spell out	In this sentence, 3 should be spelled out, as should the (sp) abbreviation Blvd. (sp)
Run in	This sentence is intentionally short. (run in) This line should not start a new paragraph: run it in instead.
Start a new paragraph	In most forms of prose, paragraphs should be fairly short. Start a new paragraph with this sentence. (¶)
Don't make the change	A line of dots under a markup symbol and the marginal note STET indicate that the change should not be made. (stet)
Query	Make a query symbol in the margin of the line where (?) your question occurs and write an appropriate query on a separate sheet. or (Qu)

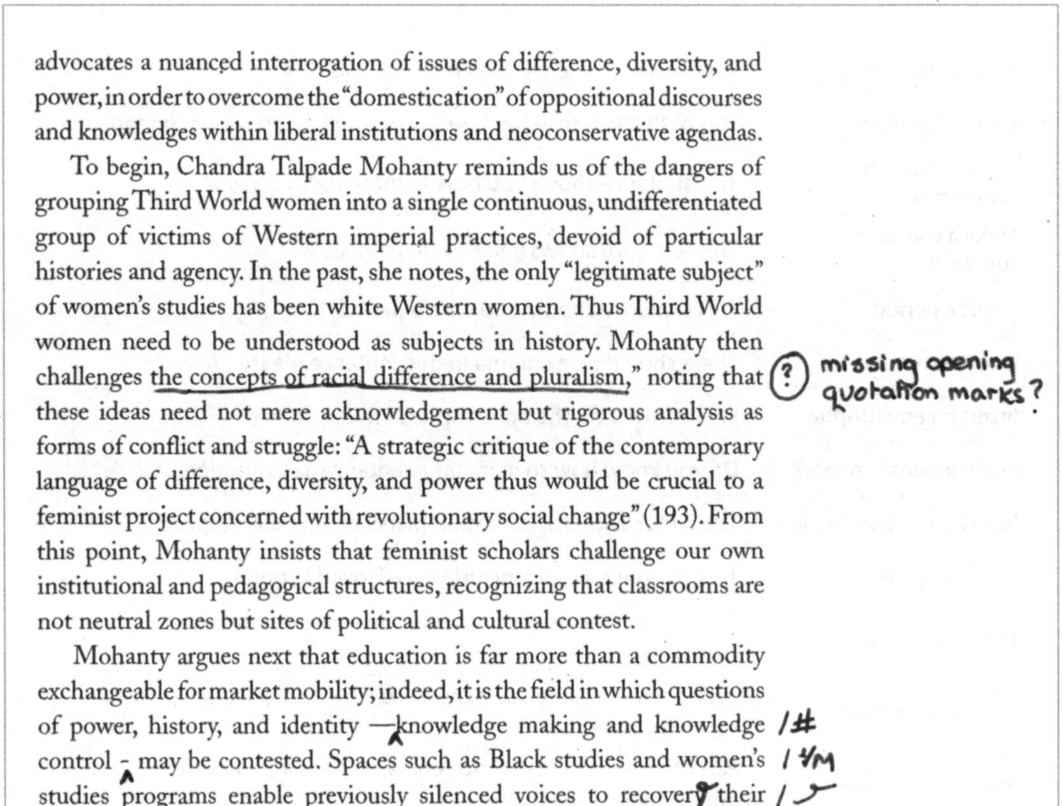

advocates a nuanced interrogation of issues of difference, diversity, and power, in order to overcome the "domestication" of oppositional discourses and knowledges within liberal institutions and neoconservative agendas.

To begin, Chandra Talpade Mohanty reminds us of the dangers of grouping Third World women into a single continuous, undifferentiated group of victims of Western imperial practices, devoid of particular histories and agency. In the past, she notes, the only "legitimate subject" of women's studies has been white Western women. Thus Third World women need to be understood as subjects in history. Mohanty then challenges the concepts of racial difference and pluralism," noting that these ideas need not mere acknowledgement but rigorous analysis as forms of conflict and struggle: "A strategic critique of the contemporary language of difference, diversity, and power thus would be crucial to a feminist project concerned with revolutionary social change" (193). From this point, Mohanty insists that feminist scholars challenge our own institutional and pedagogical structures, recognizing that classrooms are not neutral zones but sites of political and cultural contest.

Mohanty argues next that education is far more than a commodity exchangeable for market mobility; indeed, it is the field in which questions of power, history, and identity —knowledge making and knowledge control – may be contested. Spaces such as Black studies and women's studies programs enable previously silenced voices to recover their stories and empower marginalized peoples to make their own knowledge: knowledge is thus praxis. Mohanty argues that critical pedagogy requires us to rethink education, positionality and voice. Resistance is active engagement with critical consciousness, and organizing resistance can be a means by which to reclaim subjugated knowledge; but this process must happen in pedagogy and lived experience, not merely in scholarship. The recognition of the importance of lived experience is a crucial element of social transformation. Mohanty points to the rise of the "Race Industry," a conservative strategy to manage or contain anti-hegemonic or oppositional discourses such as gender, race, class, and sexuality. She argues that the homogenizing effects of this strategy must be actively and committedly resisted.

Programs such as Indigenous studies, Black studies and women's studies arose out of oppositional social movements, but were also tied to

Figure 1.2a A sample of conventional, handwritten markup.

advocates a nuanced interrogation of issues of difference, diversity, and power, in order to overcome the "domestication" of oppositional discourses and knowledges within liberal institutions and neoconservative agendas.

To begin, Chandra Talpade Mohanty reminds us of the dangers of grouping Third World women into a single continuous, undifferentiated group of victims of Western imperial practices, devoid of particular histories and agency. In the past, she notes, the only "legitimate subject" of women's studies has been white Western women. Thus Third World women need to be understood as subjects in history. Mohanty then challenges the concepts of racial difference and pluralism," noting that these ideas need not mere acknowledgement but rigorous analysis as forms of conflict and struggle: "A strategic critique of the contemporary language of difference, diversity, and power thus would be crucial to a feminist project concerned with revolutionary social change" (193). From this point, Mohanty insists that feminist scholars challenge our own institutional and pedagogical structures, recognizing that classrooms are not neutral zones but sites of political and cultural contest.

Mohanty argues next that education is far more than a commodity exchangeable for market mobility; indeed, it is the field in which questions of power, history, and identity —knowledge making and knowledge control – may be contested. Spaces such as Black studies and women's studies programs enable previously silenced voices to recovery their stories and empower marginalized peoples to make their own knowledge: knowledge is thus praxis. Mohanty argues that critical pedagogy requires us to rethink education, positionality and voice. Resistance is active engagement with critical consciousness, and organizing resistance can be a means by which to reclaim subjugated knowledge; but this process must happen in pedagogy and lived experience, not merely in scholarship. The recognition of the importance of lived experience is a crucial element of social transformation. Mohanty points to the rise of the "Race Industry," a conservative strategy to manage or contain anti-hegemonic or oppositional discourses such as gender, race, class, and sexuality. She argues that the homogenizing effects of this strategy must be actively and committedly resisted.

Programs such as Indigenous studies, Black studies and women's studies arose out of oppositional social movements, but were also tied to

7.00 x 9.00 in

12 comments

PAGE 1   12

VermeerL Nov 13
Missing opening quotation mark?

VermeerL Nov 13
✎ Highlighted Text

VermeerL Nov 13
Insert space after dash

VermeerL 2:26 PM
✎ Highlighted Text

VermeerL Nov 13
em dash

VermeerL Nov 13
✎ Highlighted Text

VermeerL Nov 13
recover

VermeerL Nov 13
T̶ Strikethrough Text

VermeerL Nov 13
insert comma

VermeerL Nov 13
✎ Highlighted Text

VermeerL Nov 13
insert comma

VermeerL Nov 13
✎ Highlighted Text

Figure 1.2b A digital version of the markup shown in figure 1.2a. Note the similarities between onscreen and paper markup.

Markup pointers

I encourage you to mark up on paper whenever you can. This suggestion may sound old-fashioned in our world of omnipresent screens, but the best proofreading happens on paper. That's partly because working on paper forces us to slow down and partly because of the way the human eye interacts with ink on paper (which depends on reflected light, unlike the emitted light of our screens). In many workflows that are otherwise digital, proofreading still happens on paper, simply because it's so easy to miss errors on the screen. Especially when we're rushing, it can be a good idea to proofread on paper because the paper is tangible and "real" in a way a digital document is not. Professional editor Allison K Williams recommends, for example, "If you're self-publishing, proofread a physical copy before putting your book on sale." Paper markup may also help the designer, who may find it slow to flip back and forth between your digital markup and the layout file.

If you mark up on paper, don't make changes to the digital file as you find errors on paper. Keep your focus on the proofreading task and mark up the full document; *then* transfer your corrections to the digital file (if it's your job to do so). Then, if possible, print out the document again to confirm that your changes are in place and no uncaught errors remain.

Although many proofreaders still review printed pages, reviewing and marking up PDF files, called SOFT PROOFING, is increasingly common, particularly in publishing workflows such as those for books and magazines. Although the work is done onscreen with a mouse and a keyboard instead of with a pencil and a stack of pages, the actual task of proofreading — slowly, carefully examining the document for various kinds of errors — is exactly the same.

When you proofread onscreen, use your tools wisely. Get to know the software and set up the toolbars in ways that are efficient for

WHERE DO ERRORS COME FROM?

We proofread to make text as close to perfect as possible before it meets its audience, not because writers are weak or incompetent. Everyone makes mistakes; every experienced proofreader has stories of errors that got past her or him. It can be helpful, however, to understand where errors come from so you can anticipate them better:

- Outright mistakes not caught in earlier passes
- Mistakes introduced during edits
- Late additions or rewrites not reviewed by an editor
- Dropped-in STANDING COPY that contains errors
- Errors made while fixing other errors on proofs

you. Enlarge the document size so the type is large and easy to read. Errors are easier to spot when they're larger, and larger type disrupts your learned "reading" process, keeping you focussed on examining words character by character. Generous sizing is also gentler on your eyes if you're looking at a screen for a prolonged period. Take frequent breaks to rest your eyes, and when you resume, start slightly above where you stopped so you get back into your flow.

Best practices in the publishing industry currently suggest that proofreaders should work on the medium in which readers will eventually consume the text: on paper for print, onscreen for digital text. More and more proofreading of all kinds is occurring onscreen, even if that's not how you proofread now. Better digital tools are making onscreen proofreading easier, and wholly digital workflows can make proofreading on paper cumbersome — and of course our world is shifting toward consuming more and more text digitally.

EXERCISE

Marking Copy

Mark the proofreading errors in the following sentences using correct markup symbols.

1. Jebediah was principal floutist of the Winnipeg Amateur Philharmonic Society.

2. A recent pole suggests photocopier rage is an issue for millions of Canadians.

3. The education ministers outrageous conduct made further discussion impossible.

4. Myrtle put her hand, over the centipede protectively.

5. Oscar Wilde wrote, "But Nature is so uncomfortable. Grass is hard and lumpy and dump and full of dreadful black insects."

6. Her laughter at that moment seemed unbarably cruel.

7. The mink farm was on the outskirts off town.

8. Giving you year-end bonus to a charitable organization will feel great.

9. What makes certain pants of speech so important?

10. The cupcakes that were siting on the counter had disappeared.

11. It is the solemnity of the ritual that make it so compelling for believers.

12. The Muggles had not been warned about werewolf lurking in the area.

13. Samson Golong brought irrefutable incidence of political interference to the attention of the police.

Whether you work on paper or onscreen, remember that the markup will be going back to a human who must interpret your work, so mark up clearly, cleanly, and consistently.

Slow it down

Probably the hardest lesson to learn about proofreading is to slow down. Proofreading is not a race, and no document is well served by frantic proofreading. It may seem counterintuitive, especially if people around you are pushing you to hurry, but proofreading slowly and methodically *saves* time. You will catch more errors in early passes when you're calm and well prepared, so you can be confident that few or no errors will emerge in subsequent passes.

Proofreading is slow work: a cursory glance at the document before you move on to the next task is *not* proofreading. You must scrutinize every character on the page, every image, every element, and you must bring the same degree of scrutiny to the last page as to the first. You cannot get bored partway through — or if you do, you must be self-aware and self-disciplined enough to stop until you regain your concentration. Some proofreaders find that physically touching each word (with a pencil or fingertip) helps them stay focussed on the task — this works well on short documents like letters and memos. But for a long, complex document, you need a plan, a space conducive to uninterrupted work, and sufficient time to take breaks to keep your attention fresh.

Slow down. As you reach the end of a document, it's tempting to rush: the end is near! But maintain your calm, slow approach and keep your standards high.

If you must proofread your own work

It is extremely challenging to proofread text that you have created yourself. Even widely experienced writers have trouble with this task and are all the more willing to let someone else help. It is also difficult to proofread text with which you are very familiar (because you have copyedited it, for instance, or because you have read it multiple times). However, the strategies in this book will help you to develop a process to bring attention to words in context and to maintain your focus on the task of examining text critically, so you can shake out any remaining errors.

One of the reasons that writers may not be the best proofreaders of their own work is purely psychological. For our own sense of self, we expect not to see errors; we tend to read past errors and see instead what we expect to read. The same psychology applies to the editor who copyedited the text. So an objective proofreader who expects to find mistakes is crucial. If you must proofread your own work, the best strategy is to gain significant distance from the text so that it becomes unfamiliar to you. Put it aside for a few weeks, or at least a few days, or you'll find yourself proofreading what you anticipate you wrote rather than what you really wrote.

Ideally even short-lived texts like social media updates and email messages would, at least in professional settings, be proofread before they are sent, but that rarely happens. If you're responsible for your organization's social media communication, you may need to proofread your own words carefully. Can you install a web browser extension or other digital tool that warns you about typos and other errors before you send a post out on social media? Can you hand your phone or tablet to someone else to proofread, particularly for missing and misused words? The "rough and ready" style of social media status updates may suggest authenticity and "being in the moment," but most professionals and organizations can't risk their credibility with avoidable typos and malapropisms. Just imagine how frustrating it must have been for the staffer who tweeted about the economic growth of the "United Sates" in July 2018!

▌▌▌▌▶BUILDING A THOROUGH PROCESS

Proofreading is contradictory work: highly detail-oriented but also superficial.
Be prepared to find errors, but moderate your touch so you're not re-performing
the work of those who have gone before you.

- Preview the document before you start proofreading. This is your preparatory
  step — don't skip it!
- Think about the purpose and longevity of the document.
- Think about the audience and its background knowledge/expectations.
- You are not re-editing the text. Look for errors, but assume the document is
  virtually finished.
- Identify the appropriate dictionary and style guide (if not assigned) and gather
  other resources as needed.
- Don't try to work without resources. You don't have to keep everything in your
  head; in fact, your brain works better when it can focus on a single task, aware
  that other tasks and content have been delegated.
- Keep a running personal style sheet where you capture local usage and styling,
  points you look up frequently in the project style guide, and other details that
  are particular to you to save yourself time and maintain accuracy.
- Use a ruler, an index card, or another eye guide to restrict your focus to a single
  line at a time.
- Make as few marks as possible to express your intentions in markup. Simplicity
  is clear and saves time.
- Divide the work into manageable sections and set priorities according to the
  time available.
- If there are digital tools you can use to assist your proofreading, use them, but
  remember that they don't replace your human eyes and intelligence.
- When you're proofreading onscreen, enlarge the display to reduce eye fatigue.
- When you're proofreading a word-processing document, change the typeface
  and type size to refresh your reading (if you can — some styling will not permit
  this kind of change).

✏▶WARMING UP TO PROOFREADING answers from page 1:

1. b. oilyliiylillyoil

2. b. 8&%8%&3&§¢8999;
   c. 8&%8%&8&§¢9999

3. c. idkjkidkjkibkkk

4. b. ?!?!?!?####!?!?!##

5. b. mmrmmmmnrnnnmnrrrr;
   c. mnrmmmmnrnnnmnnrrr

6. c. 55S555SS55S555SSS5SS

EXERCISE

Chapter I Practice

Before this reference letter is signed, it needs to be proofread. Use correct markup symbols to mark any errors.

The Modernism Appreciators Guild

14 Baez Street

New York, New York

10017 USA

Re: Maria Alicia Ipanema

To the members of the residency committee:

I have known Maria Alicia Ipanema for more than ten years. She was my student in an

English composition course when she was completing her diploma in library technology, and

almost a decade later, I was her supervisor as she competed her MA in Modernist Literature.

In these capacities, I have come to know Ms. Ipanema well: have advised her on various

matters, read her writing in a variety of genres, and watched her talent develop. She has

stayed in touch with me since her graduation and continues to mature as a creative writer.

For this reason I believe Ms. Ipanema would be an excellent candidate for a residency at the

Modernism Appreciators Guide.

   From my observation of Ms. Ipanema in class and while she was completing her

master's thesis, I feel she has both the need to work in solitude and the practical skills to get

alone successfully with others in a retreat setting. Ms. Ipanema is intelligent but also wise,

compassionate, and resilient. She is ready to find a wider creative community; given the

chance, she will become an important literary voice. She simply need an opportunity.

As the recipient of a scholarship from the University of Timmins and a bursary from the Manitoba Board of Culture and the Arts, Maria Alicia Ipanema has already been recognized locally and regionally for her talent and skill. I hope the Modernism Appreciators Guild, too, will be able to boast of Ms. Ipanema's successes, acheived with the Guild's support.

Ms. Ipanema currently works as a professional communicator, and I'm sure you recognize the cost such work can exact from a creative soul. A residency providing both peer support and dedicated time to write, reflect, and dream will allow this talented woman to purse her artistic goals and advance in her craft. Her knowledge of libraries and librarianship complements her writing skill and makes her an ideal fit with the opportunities available from the Guild.

Should you need any additional information about Maria Alicia Ipanema, please do not hesitate to contact me at (705) 555-9995. Thank you for considering this most deserving applicant.

Yours sincerely,

Joelle Lloyd-Ali, PhD

Chair, Graduate Studies

Department of Literature and Comparative Studies

University of Timmins

2

Spelling

✏️**WARMING UP TO PROOFREADING**

Do you see the error in this networking site update? *Answer on page 30.*

Fabienne Lloyd   •••
Office Administrative Professional
1 d

Having a difficult day? Take heat with this enduring wisdom:
"Living well is the best revenge." — *George Herbert*

Spelling is one of the basic checks when we proofread, and good English spelling, it is said, requires a phenomenal act of memorization. Today most writers and editors use digital tools whenever we can, and most (but not all) documents come to the proofreader after having been run through a spell-checker at some point. Still, you must recognize the limitations of the technology: digital shortcuts make the introduction of errors all too easy. Never assume that the document has been run through a spell-checker, and don't assume the spell-checker has caught all the errors in the document. The spell-checker may have been used incorrectly, or the user may have accepted a correction prompt without confirming that it was appropriate (e.g., *defiant* often shows up in place of *definite*, which is frequently misspelled as

"definate"). And of course errors may have been introduced after the spell-checker was run.

If you can run a spelling check on the document before you start proofreading, do so: it's a helpful tool. Just remember that proofreading happens at a late stage of document production, when it is sometimes too late to run the spell-checker. Also remember that spell-checking is not a substitute for your diligent proofreading. Spell-checkers, like grammar checkers, are limited in their usefulness; they support your proofreading but are insufficient in themselves. And the ubiquity of autocorrect and its often startling interjections, both on smartphones and in day-to-day word processing, should make every proofreader extra cautious.

If you do run a spelling check, keep the project style sheet handy (if you have one) and

> **Spell-checking is not a substitute for your diligent proofreading.**

make notes as you go so you don't introduce errors or inconsistencies; transfer catches to your style sheet as appropriate. Being able to spell-check a long document is helpful: at a minimum, you'll eliminate some basic errors, and if you're attentive when you're making notes, you'll notice other potential issues to watch for or gather resources for. Spell-checking a book-length Word file could take half an hour or longer: a digital process does not necessarily mean a quick process.

As this chapter explains, there are several points about spelling to consider. The number one rule is simple: don't guess! If you're not

---

✍ EXERCISE

Thinking About Spelling

Go through the following list and identify whether you believe each word is spelled correctly. If you feel a word is spelled incorrectly, write your correction in the space beside the word.

focussing _____   auxillary _____

kerb _____   enrolment _____

wont _____   foetus _____

omelette _____   practised _____

ageing _____   accomodate _____

traveler _____   adrenaline _____

realise _____   defence _____

lightbulb _____   storey _____

appendices _____   paycheque _____

villian _____   plough _____

encyclopaedia _____   yoghurt _____

glamourous _____   jewellery _____

co-operative _____   mocaccino _____

fulfillment _____   shovelled _____

humourous _____   manoeuvre _____

---

positive a word is correctly spelled, check the style sheet and then an appropriate dictionary.

Variant spellings and consistency

Spellings may vary for many reasons. In Canada, we often have to think about how Canadian spelling diverges from American and British spelling. There's a lot more to it than adding a *u* to a handful of words! Fortunately, there are resources to help you: the *Canadian Oxford Dictionary*, 2nd ed., and *Editing Canadian English*, 3rd ed. (particularly chapter 3). I've included details on these texts and other resources in appendix 5 of this book.

Spellings also vary because of writers' personal style choices (e.g., *through* versus *thru* or *perogy* versus *pirohi*). Keep in mind that variant spellings sometimes refer to specialized meanings or usage (e.g., *light* versus *lite* or *draft* versus *draught*) — check a dictionary or another resource if you're unsure.

Spellings of words that are emerging as new diction may vary (e.g., *Web site* versus *website* or *schug* versus *zhoug* or *z'hug*). So may the spellings of OPEN COMPOUNDS that are becoming common or familiar (e.g., *updo* versus *updo*; *back yard* versus *backyard*; *well being* versus *well-being* versus *wellbeing*; or *policy maker* versus *policy-maker* versus *policymaker*). Also note that the spelling of verbs that take particles (e.g., *single out, wind up*, or *break down*) usually differs from that of the noun and adjective forms of those verbs (e.g., *wipe out* [verb] versus *wipeout* [noun] or *look up* [verb] versus *lookup* [noun or adjective]). You may want to reach for a dictionary when you encounter diction like this — or at least make a note of its treatment on your style sheet. Consistency is key.

Be especially careful with proper names. There are variant spellings of many names (e.g., *Diane* versus *Dianne* or *John* versus *Jon*),

and an error involving a name is not just a spelling mistake but an error of fact. People also tend to react badly to finding their names misspelled. When possible, get source copy that verifies the spelling of individuals' names (even a business card or an online staff directory may do). You may have to query to resolve a name issue — if you can't confirm an unusual name, ask the author to confirm it. Never assume you know. Don't simply rely on the author to get details right; distinctions in spelling (e.g., *Burton Cummings* versus *Pierre Berton* or *T.S. Eliot* versus *Missy Elliott*) may not be top priority when an author is facing deadlines or juggling multiple projects. Be suspicious: assume a name may be misspelled until *you* confirm it is correct.

Consistency is one of the watchwords of proofreading. A diligent proofreader pays attention to words with variant spellings and watches for inconsistent treatments. Remember, though, that there are limits to consistency; you don't, for example, change spellings in quoted materials to conform to your style sheet.

Choosing the right dictionary for the task

If proofreading is a regular part of your workday, you need a dictionary — or perhaps multiple dictionaries — to provide authority when you must rule on spelling, usage, or other points of language. Free online dictionaries can be helpful, but many are too basic to be useful to a serious editor or proofreader. An unabridged dictionary, either printed or online (usually through subscription), is generally preferred, particularly for work in specialized areas such as medicine, law, and academia. For many professional and technical fields, you can buy dictionaries of specialized terms, which will confirm preferred spellings and meanings.

> **Be suspicious: assume a name may be misspelled until *you* confirm it is correct.**

✍ EXERCISE

Identifying Words of Concern

Read the following paragraph and circle or underline the words you would check in a dictionary or other resource if you were proofreading it.

As a genre, picture books have the ability to transcend age, reading level, and language. Although picture books are most often used with children who are pre-reading or beginning readers, a high-quality, thoughtfully rendered picture book should appeal to adults as well as students at any grade. Picture books capture this breadth of audience because they communicate on many levels. One of Canada's current stars in picture-book writing is Kyo Maclear. Her award-winning books deal with topics that are immediately relevant to children and also resonate for older readers. But the key to a successful picture book is, of course, the pictures themselves. Maclear's texts have been gracefully supported by illustrators such as Julie Morstad, Júlia Sardà, and Isabelle Arsenault. In an excellent picture book, the pictures do not simply illustrate the written text but rather complement, amplify, and even challenge it. For this reason, many picture books contain few or no words: the pictures themselves communicate the narrative. Even in picture books with substantial written texts, however, the pictures communicate a running narrative alongside the verbal story: sometimes in parallel, sometimes in opposition.

Your primary dictionary should be the one that reflects the intended audience for your documents. If your audience is primarily Canadian, the *Canadian Oxford Dictionary*, 2nd ed., is the current standard. If your audience is primarily American, *Merriam-Webster's Collegiate Dictionary*, 11th ed., and *Webster's Third New International Dictionary* are comprehensive choices. If you're working with British audiences, the *Concise Oxford English Dictionary* is the standard.

If you're working in a traditional publishing workflow, the document you're proofreading will usually conform to either a house dictionary or the project dictionary that was assigned when the text was copyedited. If you don't know which dictionary to use, ask. If you have nobody to ask, choose a dictionary wisely, according to the intended audience and the goal of creating the best document possible with the least interruption at this stage of the process. Remember not to overturn a spelling

✒ EXERCISE

Proofreading Spelling

Proofread the following sentences to catch any faulty spelling. Correct only spelling errors; query any other issues. For extra practice, use correct markup symbols.

1. My granny's house was littered with dust-catching collectables and momentos.

2. We were genuinely surprized when Dr. Fuhr took the job as departmental liason officer, but he's sure to excel in that role.

3. Melinda's on-air pronunciation was crisp, but her changable accent was a distinct liability.

4. The politician publically disavowed common vices like smoking and drinking, but partook of them regularly in private.

5. People's curiousity about Jen's tatoos makes her uncomfortable.

6. Summer tempertures sound so much cooler when expressed in Celcius degrees, don't they?

7. Have the investigators reached a concensus about whether a recurrence represents a tendancy or a trend?

8. Such miniscule differences barely register without sophisticated equipment to weigh and measure the pullets day by day.

9. The representation of party events as news led to questions about propoganda and generated sharp resistence at the annual policy convention.

10. So basicly we are stuck evaluating whether he aquired the substances accidentally or deliberately.

11. The tedium of Bert's relationship was punctuated by increasingly rare moments of ecstacy.

12. There is, of course, no problem with an ocassional argument, but escalating unresolved conflict can lead to a relationship breakdown.

13. The table at the back just ordered two mojitos, two daquiris, and a pitcher of sangria, plus a margarita pizza.

A FEW MORE SPELLING HINTS

For lists of some commonly misspelled and confused words, see appendix 3 and appendix 4 — and remember that almost every grammar or writing book on the market will include a comparable list.

- Patterns of single and doubled consonants (in words like *disappoint, accommodate, harassment*, and *millennium*) cause a great deal of confusion. You must either memorize these words or commit to looking them up every time.
- Patterns of suffixes, such as -able/-ible and -ise/-ize, also cause confusion. If you're in doubt, check.
- Watch out for silent (unpronounced) letters, unusual letter clusters, and non-standard letter order (as in *pharaoh, liaison*, and *fluorescent*).
- Watch longer words: maintain your attention through the last letter, even when you're certain you recognize the word (e.g., *accommodation* versus *accommodating* or *considerable* versus *considerate*).
- When a text introduces non-English words, you may need to check both the spelling and the mechanical treatment (that is, whether you need to treat it with italics or whether the word requires accents or special characters). Start by checking your project dictionary for guidance; in some cases, you may need to query the author.
- If you know there are specific words you struggle with, write these words in a list and keep it in a convenient place. Then, when you're proofreading, use the list to check these words easily and reinforce the correct spelling in your memory.
- Check and recheck for *pubic* used in the place of *public*. It's every communicator's nightmare, and it happens.

---

if it's correct and consistent but not one you prefer (e.g., *programme* versus *program*).

Proofreaders risk introducing errors into documents when they drop their vigilance. Especially when you're rushing or tired, it's easy to assume that a common word is what a writer intended, when really an uncommon word that looks similar is what the writer wanted — for instance, *numinous* (versus *luminous*) or *complaisant* (versus *complacent*). Such a change alters the writer's original meaning and may create confusion for readers. Be sensitive to how the writers you work with choose and use words. If you're not sure about a point in spelling or diction and can't resolve your uncertainty with your own resources, query the original writer or a colleague whose judgement you trust.

Typos and other keyboard errors

There are two typical kinds of spelling errors: outright errors and typos (which occur when a writer miskeys a word). Since we've covered the basics of misspelling, let's look at typos.

Many typos are the result of key transpositions, when the writer types a key adjacent to the intended one. Typos sometimes create viable words, which are then tough for the proofreader to discover — for instance *eager* versus *wager*, *put* versus *out*, or *precious* versus *previous*. A more complex typo occurs when the writer swaps the sequence of keys while typing a word, as in *form* versus *from*, *scared* versus *sacred*, *barely* versus *barley*, and *angel* versus *angle*. (These are sometimes called "atomic" typos, from the example of *unclear* becoming *nuclear*.) One way to catch these slips is to read the text aloud to yourself slowly, clearly pronouncing letters and syllables and listening carefully to what you're saying. The extra channel of information helps you to process what you're actually seeing and recognize mismatches. (I often run my writing through a text-to-speech utility: the computer reads my words back to me and I hear errors. This is a useful technique at the point when I know the text too well to see my mistakes.)

There is also increasingly an issue with "assisted errors," which occur when digital tools introduce errors under the guise of help. If your word-processing software or smartphone has autofill, autocorrection, or predictive tools turned on, you need to be alert for substitutions. Here are some common substitutions to watch for:

it's	←→	its
she'll	←→	shell
she'd	←→	shed
he'll	←→	hell
we'll	←→	well
we'd	←→	wed
we're	←→	were
you're	←→	your

This is a basic list; we'll look at some more startling errors in chapter 5.

It's true that we live and work in environments where errors seem all too common and we learn to "read around" mistakes almost automatically. And of course readers can usually figure out what was intended when an error occurs in print or onscreen. The omnipresence of errors today encourages some writers to argue that "good enough" is good enough. But in some cases, readers can't or won't read around minor errors — or the consequences of their judgement when they do read around errors may be severe. What impression will your readers take away if your prose is riddled with tiny, preventable mistakes? If you're trying to create the impression of a natural, spontaneous style, you *may* be able to defend *some* kinds of errors. But other choices can convey that style just as effectively without compromising correctness and quality. If your goal is to portray professionalism and to create a relationship of trust and reliability with your audience, proofreading to catch little slips matters — even on social media.

Author Philip Pullman observes that we live in an era when our language choices can be contentious. He has written at length about the writer's "responsibility towards language," a concept I believe is important for anyone who works with words. In his book *Dæmon Voices: On Stories and Storytelling*, Pullman says,

> Sometimes we come across people in our professional lives who think that this sort of thing doesn't matter very much, and it's silly to make a fuss about it. If only a few people recognise and object to a dangling participle, for example, and most readers don't notice and sort of get the sense anyway, why bother to get it right? Well, I discovered a very good answer to that, and it goes like this: if most people don't notice when we get it wrong, they won't mind if we get it right. And if we do get it right, we'll please the few who do know and care about these things, so everyone will be happy.

I think such happiness arises from accepting that we as communicators affect the reader's experience. When text flows clearly and smoothly, when it feels almost effortless to consume, readers concentrate more on our messages and less on our mechanics. I appreciate that kind of communication; I believe most readers do.

One more thing. Some spelling "errors" occur because a writer misheard a word or misunderstood what she was hearing (e.g., *phase* instead of *faze* or *peek* instead of *pique*). These confusions are learning opportunities. At a minimum, you can learn new ways to anticipate errors by figuring out other communicators' errors. And ideally, if you're in a position to share your catches non-judgmentally, you can help writers grow by pointing out confusions that mar their effective communication. But remember that one role of the proofreader is to help writers save face. In many situations you will simply fix mistakes and resolve issues without comment.

Always check instead of guessing.

Learning to spell well, and making yourself aware of spelling tricks and traps, is an investment in efficiency that can make your work easier. You'll be better equipped to catch spelling mistakes (and other proofreading errors), and although you'll be working slowly, you'll be making better catches.

The key takeaway for becoming adept at proofreading for spelling is this: get used to consulting dictionaries and other reference texts — make checking a habit rather than an exception — and always check instead of guessing.

IIII▶ BUILDING A THOROUGH PROCESS

Spelling errors can be embarrassing! Use whatever tools and resources you have to keep spelling correct and consistent.

- Use the spell-checker (carefully!) if it's available to remove any obvious spelling errors.
- Never assume the spell-checker caught all the errors or that the operator used the software correctly.
- Don't assume that a word is correctly spelled. If you're not sure, look it up! If you're still not sure, query.
- Remember that the circled instruction SP means "spell out," not "spelling error." If you find a spelling error, neatly print or type the correct spelling on the proof.
- It's *your* job to spell words correctly at this stage. Be sure to use the project dictionary and follow the style sheet.
- Resolve all spelling inconsistencies except in quoted materials (the source text must remain unchanged).
- If there appears to be a spelling error in quoted material, query it. In the published text, such errors may be marked [*sic*] to indicate that the error occurred in the source text, but this is a decision for the author or the assigning editor to make.
- Check proper names for correct spelling and consistency.
- Be cautious about letters transposed within a word and letters omitted from a word.

◔▷ WARMING UP TO PROOFREADING answer from page 23:

Note that Fabienne encourages readers to take "heat" rather than heart — an error that could easily be created by predictive text software and missed by spell-checkers and grammar checkers.

EXERCISE

Chapter 2 Practice

Proofread this list of summer events taken from an insert in a local monthly magazine. Use correct markup symbols; query anything you can't resolve yourself. All proper names are correctly spelled.

Vancouver Island Summer Guide

There's no need to leave home for fun. The Island's many festivals, cultural happenings and seasonal celebrations will keep you busy all summer long!

JUNE

Port Alice: Founders' Days

JUNE 1–2

This colorful community celebration brings residents home year after year. Live music, traditional arts and crafts sale and a duck derby for the kids. Don't miss the fireworks Saturday night, followed by a pancake breakfast Sunday morning.

Campbell River: Sea Do

JUNE 14–16

A celebration of the bounty of the Strait of Georgia. Love entertainment, food truck alley, boat show, logging skills demonstation and a dedicated kids' activity centre. Community dance Saturday evening and fireworks Sunday at midnight!

Port Renfrew: Solstice Celebration

JUNE 20–23

The Island's only sun-worship festival! Music, dancing, arts, food and family-friendly fun. Interpretive shore walks daily on the hour between 10 a.m. and 4 p.m. Be sure to sing up for the sandcastle competition!

Nanaimo: Toy Sailboat Regatta

JUNE 29–30

The world's biggest toy sailboat regatta! Gather on Newcastle Island for food, fund and hourly competitions. Onshore events include boat building for kids and educational displays on sailing, boat safety and green boating.

JULY

Sidney: Kids' Festival of Reading

JULY 2–12

The Beacon Avenue bookstores transform into an extravagant alley of book-related fun. Highlights include a Harry Potter-themed parity (July 5) and *Where the Wild Things Are* night (July 8), plus author readings and book giveaways at participating stores.

Port MacNeill: Legends of Logging

JULY 6–7

Do you have what it takes to become a legend of logging? Logging-related sprots and displays of brute strength are the focus of Port MacNeill's annual take on the Highland Games. Spectator or competitor, all are welcome. This year we have foot trucks!

Exercise continues on next page.

Port Alberni: History Fest

12–21 JULY

Celebrate the Alberni Valley's long history of fishing, forestry, farming and good living. Catch the history parade downtown Saturday, July 10, and don't miss the Indigenous education events (various locations). Enjoy a slice of our living history!

Tofino: Ocean Blues Fest

JULY 19–21

Not in its tenth year, the Ocean Blues Fest is one of Canada's best-kept secrets. This year's lineup includes Chicago Blues Reunion, MonkeyJunk, Ry Cooder, Colin James an the David Wilcox Experience, plus a dozen new legends-in-the-making.

Port Hardy: End of the Isle Music Festival

JULY 25–28

A family-friendly festival featuring Alex Cuba, Michael Franti, Captain Tractor and many local favorites. Now at a new location with lots of space for oceanside camping — or catch the shuttle from the downtown hotels. Onsite food and merch tables.

AUGUST

Parksville: Twilit EDM Festival

AUGUST 1–4

Non-stop music and light shows beginning Thursday evening, plus food vendors, arts and crafts tables and daytime beach events. Come for a day or the weekend! Admission restricted to those 19 and older.

Sidney: Beach Feast

AUGUST 3–5

More than fifty food trucks, representing everything from street food to fine dinning, will make their way to Sidney for the August long weekend. Trucks will be serving from 11 a.m. to 2 p.m. and from 5 to 9 p.m. each day. Bring you appetite!

Cowichan Bay: Bacchanalia

AUGUST 9–11

An adults-only celebration of wine and winemaking. Sample wines from across the Island and around British Columbia. Daily talks about wine appreciation, cocking with wine, wine vacations, and wine collecting. Featuring local food plus live music!

Telegraph Cove: Killer Whale Week of Welcome

AUGUST 4 TO 10

Located directly across the Broughton Archipelago from Blackfish Sound, Telegraph Cove is the place to celebrate the start of the Salmon run and the return of the resident Orcas. Education events, boat tours, art exhibitions, and more!

Ladysmith: Quietus

AUGUST 17–18

Shhh! This is a gathering especially for introverts. Features large spaces with comfortable seating for you to bring a book and read silently with others. Quite dining in dim-lit venues. Watch for book sales and themed sales tables (various locations).

Chemainus: Mini-Bard Festival

AUGUST 25–SEPTEMBER 2

A theatre festival for everyone, the Mini-Bard Festival presents dramatic readings and cut-down versions of some of Shakespeare's beat-loved plays. You haven't experienced Shakespeare until you've seen the seven-minute Hamlet!

3

Punctuation and Mechanics

 WARMING UP TO PROOFREADING

Do you see the error in this networking site update? *Answer on page 46.*

> **Blaze Cendrars**   •••
> Brand Ambassador
> 1 d
>
> Being on a design jury for the Atlantic Book Marketing Association this
> year has taught me that its nearly impossible to judge a book by it's cover.

Punctuation is another standard check for proofreaders. Writers punctuate according to conventions and to make their phrasing and expression clear. Some writers use a great deal of punctuation; some, very little. Many punctuation conventions are fairly modern (relative to the history of punctuation) and have more to do with mechanical style than with grammatically correct communication — the presence or absence of the serial comma, for instance, or the use or omission of a comma after an introductory phrase.

This chapter looks at typical issues with punctuation and mechanics (capitalization, treatment of numbers, abbreviations, and similar matters). When you proofread, consider how punctuation is used throughout the document. Consistency is important, but it never trumps clarity.

Punctuation

A few issues tend to dominate punctuation. Because the basic purpose of punctuation is to help readers understand the flow and hierarchy of information within sentences, your priority when proofreading is to uphold that purpose.

The following sections introduce key spots in text where you should anticipate problems, and then suggest how to solve them. If you need a quick refresher on basic punctuation, turn to appendix 1.

> **Consistency is important, but it never trumps clarity.**

COMMAS

These small marks cause so many problems. Here are the most common problems proofreaders encounter and some brief notes about why there are issues.

Serial comma. Often called the Oxford comma, the SERIAL COMMA appears before the conjunction in listed elements — in *beans, peas, oats, and barley*, for example. The serial comma isn't required by all styles (e.g., Canadian Press style omits it), so even if you prefer to use it, don't if the style doesn't call for it. The big issue here is consistency.

Parenthetical comma. Commas often appear in pairs within a sentence. Thus, a colleague of mine suggests you look carefully at any single comma in a sentence — it could be fine, but it could also be in need of a partner. Material enclosed in parenthetical commas could be enclosed in parentheses, or omitted from the sentence completely, without changing the meaning of the sentence or impairing its flow. The big issue here is clarity.

(**wrong**) The toddler, feeling suddenly shy covered his face and ducked behind his mother.
(**corrected**) The toddler, feeling suddenly shy, covered his face and ducked behind his mother.

(**wrong**) James Fredson who is working security at the party tonight, is Tiff's former graduate student.
(**corrected**) James Fredson, who is working security at the party tonight, is Tiff's former graduate student.

Comma splice. One of the most common grammar errors in English is the COMMA SPLICE, created when a comma by itself connects a complete sentence to another complete sentence, like this: *Jim loves to kayak, Nicole prefers canoeing.* Comma splices often crop up in prose that has been written quickly (or that is meant to represent rapid, breathless speech or thought). Fix a comma splice by creating two complete sentences; separate them with a period. You can also use a semicolon in place of the errant comma, or you can introduce a conjunction (such as *and, but, or,* or *because*). The big issues here are correctness and appropriateness for the audience.

Stray comma. Many people still believe they should insert a comma in a sentence wherever a pause would occur in speech. This idea can introduce stray commas into written language, which follows different conventions than speech does. Watch for stray commas between the SUBJECT of the sentence and its verb, or before adverbial modifiers toward the end of a sentence. The big issues here are correctness and clarity.

(**wrong**) Photographs of Jillian and her two, tiny babies were prominently displayed.
(**corrected**) Photographs of Jillian and her two tiny babies were prominently displayed.

(**wrong**) The elderly man who watches television all night, was once the governor of Idaho.
(**corrected**) The elderly man who watches television all night was once the governor of Idaho.

(**wrong**) Randy talked with me at length about his uncle's adventures, in Alaska.

(**corrected**) Randy talked with me at length about his uncle's adventures in Alaska.

COLONS

Colons are uncommon, so they tend to draw attention to themselves. There are two issues proofreaders should watch for. One is a matter of consistency, the other a matter of correctness.

Capital after colon. When INDEPEND-ENT CLAUSES are connected with a colon, some writers capitalize the first word after the colon. This is called *up style* and reads somewhat formally. Some writers prefer not to capitalize the first word after the colon; this is called *down style* and reads as more informal and accessible.

(**up style**) You have two choices: You can follow our rules or you can look for new lodgings.

(**down style**) Leonard brings important strengths to this role: he is patient, tenacious, and always willing to solve problems, no matter how challenging.

Either way, the use or absence of the capital is a point of style, not a point of grammar, so ensure the document is consistent.

Colon before object. A colon should not appear between the verb and its OBJECT or between a preposition and its object.

(**wrong**) Please bring: an entrée that can feed six, the beverage of your choice, something to sit on, and a sleeping bag.

(**corrected**) Please bring an entrée that can feed six, the beverage of your choice, something to sit on, and a sleeping bag.

(**wrong**) This election offers a choice between: what is easy and what is right.

(**corrected**) This election offers a choice between what is easy and what is right.

This point is most often an issue in lists and series, so review colon use carefully, particularly in VERTICAL LISTS (see page 44).

APOSTROPHES

Apostrophes may be misused to form plurals and are often omitted or misplaced in posses-sives. Incorrect apostrophes cause confusion and misunderstanding — *girls* versus *girl's* ver-sus *girls'*, for instance. When you proofread, check that apostrophes are correctly placed in contractions (e.g., *shouldn't, you've,* and *she's*); that plurals are not formed with apostrophes; and that the placement of apostrophes reflects possession. Also note that single opening quo-tation marks (') and apostrophes (') some-times end up interchanged:

(**wrong**) "Nice place you got 'round here," the gangster observed.

(**corrected**) "Nice place you got 'round here," the gangster observed.

It's the proofreader's job to put them right.

CONSIDER THE HYPHEN

For such tiny marks, hyphens cause disproportionate problems, mainly because writers and editors don't consistently agree on their use. What's more, hyphens present a host of problems that can be filed under different areas of proofreading: spelling, punctuation, and visual presentation. These tips about hyphens may help you keep them sorted.

The way a word breaks at the end of a line is not a matter of chance; it should relate to your project dictionary. If the hyphen doesn't directly follow a syllable, check your dictionary for guidance. You want something like *light- / house* or *photo- / graphy*, not *li- / ghthouse* or *photogr- / aphy*; otherwise, the audience may be pulled out of the text. Problems like this are often called BAD BREAKS. Here are some other examples:

- Line-end hyphenation on an already hyphenated word (e.g., *semi-auto- / matic* or *counter-clock- / wise*)
- Hyphenation of a proper noun (a specific name such as *Mac- / Donald* or *Win- / nipeg*)
- Hyphenation of a single-syllable word (e.g., *scratch- / ed* or *leng- / ths*)
- Any hyphenation that interrupts the reading experience (e.g., *the- / rapist*)

A related visual issue is STACKED HYPHENS, which refers to the appearance of a hyphen at the end of three or more consecutive lines. Proofreaders mark stacked hyphens for correction by layout staff. We will talk more about stacked hyphens in chapter 6.

The use or absence of a hyphen may change depending on the part of speech a word takes in a sentence or on the position of the word/phrase in a sentence. For example,

> Proofreaders make last-minute corrections. (A hyphen is used in a PRENOMINAL compound adjective.)
>
> *but*
>
> Proofreaders make corrections at the last minute. (The hyphen is omitted in the predicate position.)

Similar logic applies with expressions that form compounds as nouns and that form phrases as verbs. Hyphens may be involved, but with well-established forms, closed compounds are common. For example, *I read an excellent write-up on her research,* but *I'd like you to write up your findings using this form.* Here's another example: *Our cash-poor position forced the parent company to take over fiscal responsibility,* but *The takeover was rapid and unpleasant. Thank you* frequently causes trouble. For example, *I'd like to thank you for your assistance,* but *We sent a thank-you note to every guest within a week.*

If you think a document has hyphenation issues, flip through several pages, front and back, then check the style sheet before you start making major changes. The author and editor may have made intentional choices, not errors.

PLACEMENT OF PUNCTUATION

Watch where punctuation falls: there are conventions, and some choices require thought. For example, in North American English, minor punctuation is enclosed inside quotation marks, but strong punctuation (e.g., dashes, colons) is not. Punctuation around a closing parenthesis requires thought: how is the parenthetical content related to the rest of the sentence? Compare these two sentences:

> Manitoba's provincial floral emblem is the prairie crocus (*Pulsatilla ludoviciana*).

> *versus*

> Continue the exercise after three or four minutes of dancing. (You may need to remind the children of their original groups.) The second time through, ask students to imagine a process or sequence they perform regularly.

If the content inside parentheses is embedded in a complete sentence, in most cases there is no punctuation *before* the closing parenthesis. Strong terminal marks such as exclamation points and question marks, however, are usually retained.

> Many people find the fine points of proofreading extremely fussy (complicated formatting, like that found in bibliographies, may amplify this feeling).

> Ensure the solution suits the intended audience (remember, some people despise complexity!).

PAIRED PUNCTUATION

It's easy to miss one member of the pair when we write or edit with paired punctuation such as parentheses, brackets, quotation marks, and parenthetical commas. Reading text from right to left (rather than left to right as English is normally written), or reading from the bottom of the document to the top, and using a pencil or fingertip to mark and match pairs can help you find and confirm these marks. This strategy, which breaks the syntax of the sentence and isolates words and characters, will also help you find misspellings, but it won't help when you're reading for sense or looking for missing words.

MEET THE JONESES

Words that naturally end with an s and that must be made into plurals and possessives frequently give writers trouble, and sometimes confuse even proofreaders. I use the Joneses example, which isolates plurals and possessives, as a way to remember these distinctions.

> **Step 1**. Singular — One person called Jones; this is the base form: *Fawnda Jones lives in Halifax.*

> **Step 2**. Plural — Two people called Jones; add -es to the base: *The Joneses live in Halifax.*

> **Step 3**. Singular possessive — One person called Jones owns something; add 's to the base (then remove the s after the apostrophe if that's the style you're following): *Is that Tristan Jones's lunchbox?*

> **Step 4**. Plural possessive — Multiple people called Jones own something; add -es and 's to the base, then remove the s after the apostrophe: *Is that the Joneses' new home?*

The same steps apply to any s-ending noun that must be made plural or possessive.

CONFORMING TO THE STYLE GUIDE

Watch punctuation with respect to the style guide assigned to the overall project. Different style guides have different standards, and the details are sometimes finicky (particularly for documents like bibliographies). Consistency is key. Don't overrule the style guide based on your personal preference.

WATCH OUT FOR QUOTATION MARKS

The major role of quotation marks is to signal direct speech or quoted material. The conventions around direct speech are somewhat tricky. Here's a quick recap.

> "But you never took a class with Dr. Adams," Jessie observed tartly. (Note the comma at the end of the utterance, inside the quotation marks.)

> Brad announced, "I'm leaving town tonight." (Note the period at the end of the utterance, inside the quotation marks.)

> "Unless you do your homework first," Wasan replied, "you won't be going anywhere." (Note that when the speech attribution interrupts dialogue, the capitalization of the continued utterance needs attention. See the next example.)

> "Do you really like boysenberry jam?" Paul asked. "As a child, I couldn't stand the stuff." (Here both utterances are complete, so a period follows the attribution.)

In North American English, minor punctuation is enclosed inside the quotation marks; in the UK, it may appear inside or outside the quotation marks, depending on whether or not it belongs to the words within quotation marks.

North American English uses double quotation marks (" ") as the default form, while in UK English, single quotation marks (' ') are the default form, as in these examples:

> **North America**: Marie asked, "Do you remember that hockey game? I think it was in 1985."

> **UK**: Brian said, 'I neglected my dissertation because I was busy with music.'

When quotation marks are used inside of quotation marks, the opposite style is used, like this:

> **North America**: Dr. Hrynchuk said, "Mark Twain's oft-quoted quip 'Cauliflower is nothing but cabbage with a college education' turns out to be fairly accurate."

> **UK**: Dr. Meade observed, 'When Catherine exclaims, "Whatever our souls are made of, his and mine are the same", Brontë makes an essentialist claim for the entwined fates of the characters.'

Choices around how quotation marks are used involve points of style. Writers have been experimenting with other ways of indicating dialogue, but in most documents the use of quotation marks is conventional.

One point to remember: as proofreader, if you notice an error in quoted material, you must query it and not simply correct it. Sometimes this kind of error should be marked [*sic*], but that's a call for the writer or the editor.

Also, one point to watch: most typesetting today uses curly quotation marks (" " and ' ') rather than straight quotation marks (" " and ' '). Be sure curly quotation marks haven't been used in place of inch and foot marks (" and '), sometimes called minute and second marks. Also be sure a single opening quotation mark (') hasn't been used in place of an apostrophe (') — sometimes these two marks end up interchanged, and it's the proofreader's job to catch the mistake.

✎ EXERCISE

Practise Punctuating

Punctuate the word groups below, query any other issues. For extra practice, use correct markup symbols.

1. What Professor Snape the meanest teacher in the school did next was unbelievable

2. Siobhan watched the knife throwing contest interestedly after all her father had been an expert with knives

3. Imogen concluded that day to day operations shouldnt be negatively affected by last months shutdown

4. Then its off to jail with you Nefario the superhero announced triumphantly

5. No wonder its so cold in here the thermostats on the weekday setting

6. Stacy enjoyed the antics of the scotch drinking pirates at Jacks Bar last night

7. The professor asked her class What could you do to improve your composition process

8. My colleague dislikes yelling at his students hed rather stare at them until they settle down

9. Jonson wondered why the dogs had been barking in the compound yesterday

10. As it turns out however Prufrock doesnt have the strength to force the moment to its crisis

11. You have to ensure your vehicle is securely stored whenever youre away the site manager shouted

12. Wed learned several good money saving tips in Gails column the previous day

13. The panel featured three women Emma Jeela best known for her work as a showrunner Kamilla Tong a leading footwear designer and Janel Marchand an award winning sculptor and philanthropist

EXERCISE

Plural Versus Possessive

Choose the correct form of the noun in each sentence below.

1. Janetta fell in love with this (dresses / dress's) cut.

2. Simon remained an Edmonton (Oiler's / Oilers / Oilers') fan even after he moved to Germany for work.

3. This pair of (tights / tight's) already has a hole in the toe.

4. His concern with other (peoples / peoples' / people's) attitudes might be part of the problem.

5. Jerome had serious doubts about the (scissors' / scissor's) sharpness.

6. Both teams agreed to their (coaches / coach's / coaches') decision.

7. That (countries / countries' / country's) abundant natural resources remain untapped.

8. Seb started working in the (children's / childrens') section of the library right out of school.

9. Some individuals are acutely sensitive to (other's / others' / others) moods and emotional well-being.

10. Barry wished his (grandparent's / grandparents) could have attended the wedding.

11. My (family's / families' / families) celebration of the winter solstice surprises many people.

12. Sara had never liked the way that (circuses / circus's) travelled from town to town.

13. Look, Elizabeth Bennet forgot her handbag! Could we drive to the (Bennets' / Bennet's / Bennets) house and drop it off?

Mechanics

In the context of punctuation, MECHANICS refers to conventions reflecting typographical standards for treatment — for instance, how numbers are represented or how the titles of works are included in prose. Style guides speak loudly here. Most of the conventions exist to help readers quickly understand unusual inclusions or to recognize distinctions such as proper names and abbreviations. Such matters should be groomed for consistency: consistency is a convention of fine attention that makes text feel clean and reliable.

CAPITAL LETTERS

Capital letters have a few functions in written English. In prose, every new sentence begins with a capital letter. An initial capital marks a proper noun or proper adjective, including most personal, organizational, and proprietary names, as well as a small group of official or honorary titles (e.g., the Queen, the President, the Big Apple, Toronto the Good — the capital is a signal of respect). All caps is sometimes — rarely — used for emphasis, but if you pay attention you'll observe that most edited English prose contains few capital letters. So scrutinize any word that starts with a capital letter: if it's not the first word of a sentence, it's likely either a proper name (a person, a place, a company, a brand) or an error.

Writers tend to overuse capitals. Sometimes they are imitating forms they have seen in other settings (e.g., capitalizing the names of seasons or cardinal directions, which in most cases don't need a capital). Sometimes they are communicating significance or respect (e.g., capitalizing jobs or roles, which in most cases don't need a capital). An assigned style always trumps personal preference, though, so if your client or organization follows a style guide, you must follow it consistently.

Pay close attention when you're working with content about Indigenous Peoples or by Indigenous authors. Words may be capitalized in this context that wouldn't take a capital in other settings (e.g., Longhouse, Sweat Lodge, Chief, Elder, Survivor, Protocols). This is an intentional choice, says Gregory Younging, author of *Elements of Indigenous Style*: "It is a deliberate decision that redresses mainstream society's history of regarding Indigenous Peoples as having no legitimate national identities; governmental, social, spiritual, or religious institutions; or collective rights." If you're uncertain about these capitals or their consistency, query them rather than changing them and check in with the author or the assigning editor.

Titles of works can be particularly troublesome. You must think about both capitalization of the words in the title and whether those words should be italicized or enclosed in quotation marks. Except when you're using specific style guides (such as APA), capitalize all major words, including articles (*a, an, the*) when they are the first word of the title. This style is called *title case*. Omit capitals on prepositions that are less than five letters long, as well as on short conjunctions (*and, but, or, for,* etc.) and articles. Here are a few examples:

"I Fought the Law"

The Sun Is Also a Star

Julien Levy: Memoir of an Art Gallery

"Fell in Love with a Girl"

In the Midst of Winter

On Our Street: Our First Talk About Poverty

"Sky Full of Song"

If you capitalize only the first letter of the first word and any proper names in the title, the style is called *sentence case*. It is much less common than title case.

If you work with documents that are divided into multiple sections (e.g., textbooks, technical reports, or academic articles), you may need to think about the capitalization of titles regularly, as headings and different levels of subheading may follow different formats. For example, the title block and the top-level

EXERCISE

Capitalization

Capitalize the following document correctly. Query any other issues.

---

attn: amanda bedelya

sosevere social sciences and humanities publishing
909 east queen elizabeth parkway
toronto, on m5w 2n1

re: dissertation royalties

please find enclosed two copies of a form that was sent to me last week. the form pertained to me but is addressed to someone else's name at my home address. in the past sosevere has sent small royalty payments to me at this address using my correct name, and i suspect an error has been introduced into your system. my letter is intended to correct that error.

although the enclosed forms bear the name "beatrice quimby," they should be made out to "wilhemina fosse." my dissertation, *the essential made concrete in the poetry of robert kroetsch*, was defended in the department of english, faculty of arts, at the university of edmonton in 2010. the address on havitur way in shackleton, saskatchewan, is the only one you should have on file for me, as it is my permanent home address and has been for more than a decade.

again, in the past, sosevere has correctly issued small payments to me with respect to my dissertation's use. in 2018, however, i submitted a revenue canada tax disclosure form at sosevere's request, and i suspect there was a processing error with that form that has led to the misidentification on the forms i have enclosed. since the sum involved this year appears to be zero dollars and zero cents, there is presumably little urgency to this correction, but for the sake of records and my continued academic publishing, i need to know that this error has been corrected.

i look forward to receiving your written confirmation that the correction has been made; in the meantime, i have retained one copy of your form in case i need it.

if you should need to reach me directly, please call me at 306-555-9090. thank you for your prompt attention to this matter.

sincerely,

dr. wilhemina fosse
associate professor
department of english
university of saskatoon
c/o 123 havitur way
shackleton, sk s0s 0n0

subhead might use title case, but lower-level subheads might use sentence case (and other formatting may also be involved, such as the introduction of bold or italics or the depth of line indentation — another element to keep consistent). All caps is also an option, as you see in some headings in this book.

TREATMENT OF NUMBERS

With numbers, you must think about the treatment and consistency between the number (expressed as a word or words) and the numeral (expressed as a digit or digits). The rules for treatment can be fairly straightforward or extremely complicated — just think of all the ways we express numbers in speech and writing. Your task as proofreader is to ensure the chosen style (e.g., APA, Canadian Press, MLA) has been applied consistently and appropriately. The styling decision is made by the copyeditor, but the inconsistent treatment of numbers is a common problem proofreaders encounter. (If you want a deep dive on the many ways to treat numbers, check out the *Chicago Manual.*)

As a baseline, the simplest styling spells out numbers zero to nine and uses digits for 10 and above. If a number is spelled out, any accompanying units are usually also spelled out (e.g., six litres of milk). If a number is expressed in digits, accompanying units may be either spelled out or abbreviated, depending on the overall style guide (e.g., 500 miles, 398 mL). In the interest of readability, a number and its unit should be treated as a block and should not be separated at a line end or page turn. Here's one firm rule to commit to memory: when a sentence begins with a number, it is expressed in words, irrespective of the document's overall style.

Never forget that humans, not machines, will read the eventual text: think about how to make the text readable, usable, and meaningful when numbers are involved. For instance, use digits in recipes and process documents for quick, easy understanding.

ABBREVIATIONS AND ACRONYMS

Abbreviations and acronyms are common in scientific and technical writing and in certain kinds of corporate communication. When you're dealing with abbreviations and acronyms, several issues arise. Consistency is primary, but correctness and clarity also demand your attention.

Watch the use of punctuation with abbreviations. In North American English, most abbreviations take a period to signal the missing letters, but not all do. Notably, metric (SI) symbols never take periods. Be sure the abbreviation itself is correctly spelled. If a word has been abbreviated after its first instance (e.g., *socioeconomic status*, normally abbreviated *SES*), be sure to maintain its abbreviation throughout the document.

With acronyms, be sure the full name of whatever the acronym refers to occurs somewhere in the document. Different style guides have different standards for how to handle this point. Also be sure the acronym is correctly and consistently treated with or without periods (often called "points" in this context) and spelled properly (e.g., don't let BIOL become BOIL at some point). Check carefully: many spell-checkers ignore words in all caps, including abbreviations and acronyms.

Abbreviations and acronyms may be formatted with SMALL CAPS, a special type of treatment that stands out on the page. Here are a few examples with and without small caps:

a CBC personality
a CBC personality
new W3C standards
new W3C standards
ARIA attributes
ARIA attributes
our UNICEF representative
our UNICEF representative

Many editors recommend against using small caps in technical documents, so be sure you know the expectations for the project you're working on.

Another common mechanical issue involves the treatment of provinces, states, and other elements of addresses. In running text, spell these elements out (e.g., the capital of New Brunswick; Highway 16; Monteith Road; near the Montana border). In address blocks, use postal abbreviations (e.g., Fredericton, NB; HWY 16; Monteith RD; Cooke City, MT). Note that some style guides (e.g., the *Chicago Manual*) prefer standard abbreviations rather than postal abbreviations in tables and display text. You may need to check your project style guide or another resource.

One of the most commonly confused abbreviations is the representation of a.m. (*ante meridiem*) and p.m. (*post meridiem*) in expressions of time. The *Chicago Manual* recommends editors use periods and lower case, but acknowledges that the periods may be omitted and the type styling could be small caps (but not full capitals). Once again, consistency is key. The copyeditor likely chose a style; be sure it has been consistently applied.

VERTICAL LISTS

When editors talk about lists, they are often referring to in-line lists, which are integrated into complete sentences. But sometimes a list is displayed apart from a paragraph to draw attention to its contents; this is called a VERTICAL LIST.

A vertical list involves many of the elements this chapter has discussed, and there are many ways of handling these elements, depending on the content and the context. Treatment decisions will have been made by the copyeditor, informed by the appropriate style guide. Beyond basic correctness, you are looking for consistency in several features:

- bullets (if used)
- punctuation following letters/numbers when they are used to introduce listed items

- case of letters when they are used to introduce listed items
- case of the first word of listed items (other than proper names)
- punctuation (if any) following listed items
- hierarchy (if any listed items include subpoints)
- any other type formatting (e.g., bold or italics on subheads that lead into listed items)

Remember that ordinary bullets (em dashes, asterisks, circles, arrows) imply that the ordering of the listed items is inconsequential. Letters or numbers in front of listed items imply that the sequence or the hierarchy matters. Be sure all the numbers/letters are present and correctly sequenced (see figure 3.1).

Listed items are generally presented using PARALLELISM. If they are not parallel, a proofreader might make this change if they have the authority; otherwise, they should query.

ITALICS

Italicized type has many functions in written English, and your job as proofreader is to know what should and should not be italicized. The most significant role of italics is to draw emphasis to a word or phrase: the change in the type slows a reader down and makes the reader pay attention. Italics are also applied to words used as terms or to draw the reader's attention to a word used as a word (e.g., the word *word*). You'll notice, for example, that throughout this book, words are italicized when I refer to them as names for concepts or processes. Italics may be used on non-English words and phrases that have not been anglicized and are still considered "foreign" (e.g., *bonjour* takes italics, but *tête-à-tête* doesn't); this status and conventions around how to handle it change as the language evolves, so consult your project dictionary or style guide for assistance. If it's in your dictionary without

These twelve nations are expected to have the largest economies by 2024:

a. United States of America

b. People's Republic of China

c. Japan

d. Germany

e. United Kingdom

f. India

g. France

h. Brazil

j. Canada

k. South Korea

l. Russia

These are the thirty Canadian writers whose work appears most frequently on outlines in Canadian literature courses between 2001 and 2016:

Atwood, Margaret
Blais, Marie-Claire
Blunt, Giles
Brand, Dionne
Crummey, Michael
Davies, Robertson
Donoghue, Emma
Engel, Marian
Ferguson, Will
Juby, Susan
King, Thomas
Laurence, Margaret
Leacock, Stephen
MacDonald, Ann-Marie
Martel, Yann

Mitchell, W.O.
Montgomery, L.M.
Moore, Lisa
Mootoo, Shani
Mowat, Farley
Munsch, Robert
Munro, Alice
O'Neill, Heather
Pearson, Kit
Richler, Mordecai
Robinson, Eden
Smart, Elizabeth
Toews, Miriam
Urquhart, Jane
Winter, Kathleen

According to Veldkamp's survey, these are the most common errors of grammar and composition:

1. Comma splice

2. Apostrophe misuse

3. Sentence fragment

4. Dangling modifier

5. Subject/Verb disagreement

6. Diction misuse

7. Pronoun/Antecedent disagreement

9. Misplaced modifier

8. Stray commas

10. Vague/Absent antecedent

11. Run-on sentence

12. Split infinitive

Figure 3.1 Check content presented in vertical lists for completeness and correct alphabetical or numerical ordering. In the first example, note that the list contains only eleven nations and item "i" is missing. In the second example, note the alphabetizing error with Munro and Munsch. In the third example, note the numbering runs 9 to 8 rather than 8 to 9.

italics, then use it without italics. If it's not in the dictionary, use italics. Finally, the titles of long works or works that are complete in themselves — books, magazines, movies, and paintings, for instance — are italicized. (The titles of smaller works such as poems and songs are normally enclosed in quotation marks; do be aware that some style guides contradict these basic rules.)

Italics in typography replace the function of underlining in handwritten text or text typed on a typewriter. For that reason, underlining tends to be uncommon in typeset copy. Examine any underlined text carefully: it should probably be treated as italic, but if you're in doubt, query.

Keep in mind mechanical choices that are specific to disciplines, such as the use of italics on species names (e.g., *Betula alba* ssp. *excelsa* [Aiton] Regel, otherwise known as the paper birch). In professional and academic discourses, adherence to these mechanical forms is almost as important as the accuracy of the information itself.

IIII▶BUILDING A THOROUGH PROCESS

As with spelling, if you're not sure whether a point in punctuation is correct, check; don't guess. Don't add or delete punctuation only because of the way the sentence sounds to your mind's ear. Think instead about what will be clearest to readers. With practice, your sense of punctuation will become confident and graceful. You'll know where there's licence in the rules and conventions, and you'll recognize where a choice may distract the audience from the message.

- Be sure every sentence begins with a capital letter and ends with terminal punctuation (a period, a question mark, an exclamation point, or ellipsis points).
- Watch for consistent comma use (serial comma included or omitted).
- Ensure colons have been removed from the ends of headings and subheadings.
- Review any materials where punctuation is applied repeatedly (e.g., in vertical lists; read similar materials side by side to find inconsistencies).
- Ensure abbreviations and acronyms are written out in full at first instance (unless that is not the practice of your style guide).
- Remove extra spaces, particularly after terminal punctuation: only one space is needed between sentences.

✏▶WARMING UP TO PROOFREADING answer from page 33:

Note the misplaced apostrophes. This text should read "Being on a design jury for the Atlantic Book Marketing Association this year has taught me that it's nearly impossible to judge a book by its cover."

EXERCISE

Chapter 3 Practice

Proofread this excerpt from a magazine article about twentieth-century writer and artist Mina Loy. Pay particular attention to punctuation and mechanics; query any other issues.

Dada Arthur

Arthur Cravan, born Fabian Avenarius Lloyd on May 22, 1887 was a wholly original Modernist. A nephew of Oscar Wilde, he aggressively rejected conventional society. He travelled widely as a young man, throughout Europe, and across America, making his way by picking up odd jobs and boxing. He is best remembered today as the pugilistic forefather of the Dada movement who once said, "Let me state once and for all: I do not wish to be civilized".

One of Cravan's many proto-Dadaist exploits involved preparing a French-language magazine (*Maintenant* — "Now") of his work in his own hand-writing and selling it on the streets of Paris from a wheelbarrow. He published 5 issues, made up entirely of his own writing plus illustrations form various French artists. He delivered a lecture at a learned society that he opened by firing a pistol into the air. He then preceded to make provocative statements about art, culture, and life, then concluded by throwing his briefcase at the apparently wrapt audience.

Perhaps, his most outrageous performance involved his offer to kill himself in front of an audience to placate those who were offended by his taunting and criticism. The event was scheduled for a local bar; Cravan promised to lecture in a jock strap (to please the ladies, *bien sûr*) and drink Absinthe as he perished. But when the crowds — and the reporters — showed up, Cravan harangued the public for their tawdry tastes (how gauche to show up for a suicide!), then gave a highly-conventional presentation about French writer, Victor Hugo.

Mina Loy met Arthur Craven in New York in April 1917, and they were instantly attracted to each other. They were married less than a year after meeting. The couple spent the early part of 1918 bumming across Mexico, desperately poor but also fiercely in love. By July Mina was pregnant, and the couple decided to return to Europe.

They had to little money to travel together, so Mina sailed to Buenos Aries to wait for Arthur, who was to follow a few days later. But Arthur disappeared and was never heard from again, he was presumed lost at sea. Arthur's disappearance marked a crucial turn in Loy's life.

4

Grammar

✏️ **WARMING UP TO PROOFREADING**

Do you see the error in this networking site update? *Answer on page 55.*

 Fabienne Lloyd
Office Administrative Professional
1 d
• • •

When things get tough, we often talk about having the "grit" to carry on. But what is grit?
Here's my definition: Grit is the raw endurance, determination, and drive that keeps you
going despite the barriers people set before you.

Grammar and usage are the third standard check of proofreading. Although most grammar errors should have been caught during earlier editing processes (the copyediting stage, if you follow a traditional publishing workflow), a few may remain. Sometimes they are artifacts of the editing process itself. Sometimes they're tricky points in grammar that both author and editor missed. Regardless of why they remain, grammar errors demand thoughtful attention.

As proofreader, you are responsible for correcting egregious and confusing grammar errors. But what is "egregious" at this stage is, to some degree, a matter of opinion. Let's look at two fairly common types of errors.

Errors in subject–verb agreement are common in composition and are normally caught during copyediting. Sometimes, though, they're missed or even introduced during editing — for instance, if a subject is changed from plural to singular and the verb is not changed accordingly. Subject–verb disagreements are highly visible errors and thus are rarely allowed to stand on proofs because they tend to pull readers out of their reading.

Another common error at the proofreading stage involves the presence of a pronoun like *this, it,* or *which* as the subject of a clause when the pronoun reference is vague. In the sentences below, for example, the pronouns lack clear referents; they refer instead to the general *idea* of the preceding clause:

Agriculture can produce enough food to feed more than seven billion people, but the food is badly distributed across the world. *This* is why local food security is so important.

From Edson to the Jasper park gates, the snow kept falling, *which* made driving exhausting.

✍ EXERCISE

Subject and Verb Agreement

Choose the correct form of the verb in each sentence below.

1. The board of trustees (select / selects) a chair after the election results have been confirmed.

2. Investigators soon realized bacteria (was / were) responsible for the product discoloration.

3. Either the institution or the individual scientists (present / presents) findings at the next session.

4. Under an unimaginably blue sky complemented by verdant hills on three sides (sit / sits) Old Joe's trapping cabin.

5. The opinion of advertisers and/or their ownership (does / do) not reflect the view or endorsement of the publisher.

6. The sound of his approaching footsteps (reminds / remind) me that I need to leave.

7. There (is / are) more granola bars in the pantry.

8. Each of the scholarship winners (was / were) called to the stage to be recognized.

9. Masking all of this (is / are) flat wages and disappearing benefits.

10. A long list of nominees for this year's Giller Prize (has / have) been announced.

11. Neither the class nor the teacher (was / were) happy with the test scores.

12. The biggest issue (is / are) the complaints about cold food we hear during peak hours.

13. A council drawn from top industry leaders (has / have) been invited to examine rates.

Unlike subject–verb disagreements, vague pronoun references may not be corrected on proofs — depending on the sentence and the publisher, of course — because many readers do not notice vague references. All of this is to demonstrate that proofreading grammar is not entirely clear-cut. You may have to query some constructions and may even let some errors stand. Your good judgement during this stage of the process is crucial.

Unless you have advanced knowledge of grammar and usage, I recommend you avoid running a grammar check. Less-experienced users can introduce errors into writing under the guise of checking grammar: the grammar checker often works like a sledgehammer where a chisel is needed. Well-trained editors are likely to know more about grammar than online tools or software applications do, so if your grammar is still wobbly, tread lightly and invest your energy in reading, research, and practice. (If you need a quick refresher on basic grammar, turn to appendix 2.) Thus, whether you fix a grammar issue or query it may come down to your good judgement, your local process, your authority as proofreader, and the significance of the document.

What you're seeking when you proofread for grammar

If you're working alongside a writer and an editor, proofreading grammar can be challenging. What we commonly think of as "grammar" issues are actually a blend of questions and judgements about diction, dialect, usage, and register — not to mention clarity of phrasing and personal style. Please resist the temptation to overreach your authority as proofreader and change another person's expression (or even your own) at this stage. Let's consider a few points.

The standards of "good" grammar exist on a spectrum, and writers position themselves, consciously or unconsciously, along that spectrum as the meeting place between the authorial voice or persona and the audience. They do so by accepting and rejecting conventions and choices such as which word to use, how to phrase a sentence, how formal or informal to be, and how personal or impersonal to be. Even unsigned, functional prose — think information on a municipal website or the fine print in a purchase agreement — has a sound that positions the content relative to the potential readers. As the proofreader, your role is to uphold that positioning — or to point out where it slips. But remember: at this stage, you are marking outright mistakes only.

What's appropriate for one audience may not be so for another. You should be proofreading sensitively enough to observe when something has been done for effect (which you gauge by watching for patterns and observing clues in the text) and when something is an error. If the same choice has been made repeatedly, it's probably intentional (or else a consistent error). You should be able to judge whether the writer's choices suit the intended readership, not so you can rule for or against them but so you can make congruent decisions when you offer corrections and queries. Don't be hasty; read enough of the text to make a fair judgement *before* you start changing the document.

Thus, in writing that's intended to be approachable, fresh, and short-lived, you might expect to see fragments and short sentences, split infinitives, contractions, some slang, some loose use of *you* and *your*, and other markers of informal writing. In sell copy, for instance, or newsletter content, this style must be balanced by standards of correctness that demonstrate

> **You should be able to judge whether the writer's choices suit the intended readership, not so you can rule for or against them but so you can make congruent decisions when you offer corrections and queries.**

✍️ EXERCISE

Modifiers

Review the sentences below. If a sentence contains an error, rewrite it. For extra practice, use correct markup symbols.

1. Moving here, there, and everywhere, the constants in my life have been my family and my painting.

2. Elmer feels badly about running into you with his bike.

3. The silverskin should be left intact when cooking ribs on the barbecue.

4. While running to catch the LRT, my phone fell out of my pocket.

5. The kicker barely moved the ball seven yards.

6. When starting work as an apprentice meat cutter, the expectations may be confusing and the hours long.

7. This perfume, even under its generic, off-label copy name, would smell just as sweetly.

8. When used as directed, allergic reactions are rare.

9. This was a devastating fire for a lot of people that did not need to occur.

10. We enjoyed a real tasty sundae at the diner the other day.

11. I decided after I saw Arthur I would never smoke again.

12. A portion of the proceeds from the sale of this book will go to a memorial fund for victims of Hurricane Maria and the University Music Department.

13. After today, this behaviour is going to absolutely and without question stop.

professionalism, competence, and care. In creative writing, "poor" grammar may be a deliberate stylistic device. On the other hand, in writing meant for permanence or making a serious statement — a legal opinion, a government policy, or a dissertation, for example — you might expect conventional choices, long sentences, sophisticated diction, and polished grammar. This style is correct and competent but also speaks to the highly specialized needs of its audience.

If a correction is obvious, make it: that's your job. If a correction will involve recasting or rewriting the sentence, think carefully about process. Are you looking at a genuine error? Does it cause confusion or otherwise interfere with communication? What does the audience expect and need? What has the writer created? What can you do as proofreader, without trespassing on other roles, to keep the connection between writer and reader secure?

Usage and correctness

Many of the slips we call grammar errors are really *usage* issues. Usage as a linguistic concept refers to the way a language is used day to day — it's a measure of a living language.

Use your judgement. Editors tend to be fairly permissive about language; they generally support writers as they experiment and play with language. But editors also tend to be trained in traditional or "prescriptive" language rules, so are prepared to uphold more conservative language traditions when it's appropriate to do so. Remember that language is alive, and "rules" change over time. For example, most editors today wouldn't worry about a split infinitive ("to boldly go"), a sentence that ends with a preposition ("Where are you from?"), or a possessive formed with an inanimate object ("the clock's incessant ticking" instead of "the incessant ticking of the clock"), but all of these examples were once points for editorial intervention (and pedantic outrage).

Informal language and slang

English is a living language. Its users keep it alive by creating new meanings for words or using words in unusual ways, as well as by creating new words to describe new objects, experiences, and actions. It is also an international language, and users bring their dialects and backgrounds to the immediate writing situation. Nowhere are these features more noticeable than in the use of informal language and slang in writing.

If you encounter a word or phrase you're unfamiliar with that seems plausible in context but doesn't appear in your dictionary, use a search engine to check its preferred spelling (and competing spellings, if they exist), its meaning, and its typical usage. If the results are unsatisfactory or suggest the word/phrase is just an error, then query it.

Examples of such usage that are current in the early 2020s are *judgy* (or *judgey*, both lending an ironic edge to the more staid *judgmental*) and *bougie* (or *boujee*, both derogatory derivations of *bourgeois*). Recognize, though, that such inclusions depend on audience. Not every user of a language adopts changes at the same rate, and slower adopters may rail against some informalisms and slang. As a very divisive example, consider *literally*, which literally means "to the letter" — that is, it describes or applies to something actual and exact (e.g., *The climber was literally at the end of her rope* versus *He is literally the last person I would ask for help*). Increasingly, though, *literally* is used in a figurative sense, to the point that at least one dictionary now defines *literally* to mean figuratively. This shift could be a source of amusement or of despair, depending on your views on usage.

Thoughts about usage bring us quickly to *register*. Register refers to the level of formality a document displays. Some documents are chatty and informal, like a conversation with a friend or a stinging gossip columnist; some are highly formal, even stuffy, because that's what's expected of them. The more formal the document, the less freedom the writer has to deviate from the style of language called Standard English (or Standard Edited English). The less formal and more personal the document, the more the writer might adopt informal diction and slang — assuming, of course, that such a choice won't alienate the audience. Remember that slang marks its users as belonging to the "in" group that understands fast-changing diction. As proofreader, you usually don't have the authority to change diction to conform to register, but you should query anything that pushes you out of the document or that seems out of place for the anticipated purpose or audience.

But the rules!

All proofreading takes place in a real context where time and money are finite and where power and politics sometimes overrule a proofreader's knowledge and skills. Few people like to have their language corrected, and many people are fiercely loyal to "rules" they learned in grade school. (Theodore M. Bernstein calls these "hobgoblins": rules such as not ending a sentence with a preposition, not starting a sentence with *because*, and always placing a comma after an introductory phrase.)

You will encounter clients and colleagues who insist something wrong is actually right — often because they have erroneously internalized a rule or because it "sounds" right to their ear despite the grammar. These are always difficult situations, especially in small organizations. How high are the stakes? Will this choice besmirch the credibility of the document or the individual or the organization? If you're going to try to persuade someone in this situation, marshal your resources. Consult a grammar book, bookmark several authoritative websites, get an explanation from a colleague whose authority is respected — but also consider whether this issue is really a hill to die on. Although you may catch points like these when you're proofreading, think carefully about context before you correct them and recognize that correcting them may require considerable tact. In some cases, it's better to let the writer be "wrong" than to engage in an extended and unwinnable fight; in most cases, thoughtful conversation can allow everyone involved to save face and look professional.

IIII▶ BUILDING A THOROUGH PROCESS

As with spelling and punctuation errors, grammar mistakes occur because writers are juggling the tasks of forming ideas and expressing those ideas simultaneously — often while other activities happen in the writer's background. Writers can't always perceive their own slips; that's why they may need other sets of eyes to ensure their documents communicate effectively. Grammar errors may also be introduced during editing processes — and that's why we proofread.

- Fix all obvious agreement issues: pronouns should agree with ANTECEDENTS and verbs must agree with subjects.
- Be sure modifiers have a clear relationship to what they modify.
- Confirm all possessives and plurals are correctly formed: scrutinize apostrophes (or their absence).
- Confirm parallelism.
- Keep diction and usage appropriate to the document's purpose and audience.

WARMING UP TO PROOFREADING answer from page 49:

Note the agreement of the COMPOUND SUBJECT *raw endurance, determination, and drive* requires a plural verb, *keep*.

✍️**EXERCISE**

Chapter 4 Practice

Proofread the following poster, which is intended for a community notice board. Make whatever changes are needed; query anything you can't resolve yourself. For extra practice, use correct markup symbols.

We're Looking To Score With You!

Portage la Prairie Womens Floor Hockey League

Have you wanted to play floor hockey since leaving school? We do too! Join us every Thursdays for a fun "beer league" experience!

Thursdays, 8:45 to 9:55 pm.
(please arrive at least 5 minutes early and
changed and ready to play—there are locker rooms on site)

Sept 6 - Dec 20 and Jan 3 –May 30
Portage Community Sportsplex, 30 Dauphin Drive

$20 per drop-in (cash only) or $550 for the whole season

No experience necessary
Bring your own plastic stick (available from Cdn Tire). Pucks and pinnies provided.

For more information please call or text

Sara Lamiroden @ **204-555-1212**.

Women only, 19+

5

Proofreading to Make Sense

✏️ WARMING UP TO PROOFREADING

Do you see the error in this networking site update? *Answer on page 67.*

Blaze Cendrars
Brand Ambassador
1 d

• • •

I just saw this information posted about an old pal: "During her 20-year tenure (1998–2008) coaching the Ontario Climbing Association's junior team, Darcy Dut inspired thousands of young people to greater heights." Wow!

As we have established, the proofreader's job is to check that what will be published not only is correct and consistent but also says what the author intended. For that reason, you must confirm that the text makes sense both as a whole and in its parts. Proofreading for sense is challenging because your brain must move rapidly between the macro and the micro. The most important idea about proofreading for sense is to *slow down*.

Our brains can catch mechanical errors quickly, but finding errors in logic is more difficult and requires reflection. For instance,

> Research shows that despite our cynicism about the exam process, the actual likelihood of an evaluator completely missing the mark on a blind evaluation is actually pretty low.

The most important idea about proofreading for sense is to *slow down*.

Did you notice the repetition of *actual* (in *actually*) in this sentence? If you did, excellent! That's the kind of attentive, reflective reading this task demands. (A funnier version of this kind of error was at one point regularly making the rounds on social media: "The Flat Earth Society has members all around the globe.")

Missing and misused words

As you proofread for sense, think carefully about words. Are the words you see the correct words, or were other words meant — that is, has a similar-sounding or similar-looking word been substituted? Has a word been used appropriately in context — for instance, should it be the noun form or the adjective form (e.g., *satisfaction* or *satisfactory*)? Do the words appear in the correct order? Have words been repeated or omitted? You must evaluate

✍ **EXERCISE**

Training Your Attention

This exercise asks you to think carefully about words. Make whatever proofreading changes are necessary. For extra practice, use correct markup symbols.

1. There are structural problems with the novel, notably some repetition and several saggy passages in the novel.

2. For professional communicators, liable — a lasting form of defamation — is an ever-present risk.

3. Beware of one editorial foible: editors want everything to be right and tend to stress needless about insignificant copy.

4. In British Columbia, prosecutors are referred to as Crown council.

5. Hormones increase or inhabit how quickly cells perform their ordinary functions.

6. We are alarmed to learn that the person in question has developed still more disruptive behavioural ticks over the past year.

7. Most breeders for the ornamental plant industry, worth some $40 billion globally, simply ignore the fragrant of flowers, preferring instead to focus on high-value qualities like colour and vitality.

8. Lately it's rare to read a business story and not discover some marquis organization announcing layoffs or an earnings downgrade.

9. The world *tattoo* derives from a Tahitian word, *tatu*, meaning "to mark something."

10. The first blacksmiths in Lower Fort Garry were English, imported specifically by the Hudson Bay Company.

11. Everyone was embarrassed at discovering the couple in the throws of passion.

12. Always review your writing carefully to check whether you have any words.

13. His grandfather had put up thirty pounds for third-class passage to Canada on the Norddeutscher Lloyd liner *Prinz Heinrich*.

meaning as well as presentation: words may be correctly spelled and punctuated, but if they're the wrong words in the setting, that could be a serious error.

Language creates sense from units of meaning, so use natural units to your advantage. Read verb phrases *as* phrases to confirm form and tense: for example, *could go, could have gone, could have been going* — you may need to rebuild the verb phrase if it's embedded in a question or separated by modifiers. Look for the tense marker and any AUXILIARIES (*can, could, shall, should, will, would, may, might, must,* or forms of *be, have,* or *do*). For example, in the sentence that follows, the verb phrase has been inverted with the subject (*a government*) and interrupted by a modifier (*similarly*). The tense is marked by *has*; both tense and meaning would be altered if *had* replaced *has* or if part of the verb phrase were missing.

> When prior to the decriminalization of cannabis <u>has</u> a government <u>been</u> similarly <u>tasked</u> with simultaneous judicial, health policy, and public relations issues?

Similarly, read prepositional phrases *as* phrases: mentally (or physically) mark the preposition, especially if it's only two or three letters, and find its object; then confirm it's an appropriate preposition for the situation. (Selecting prepositions can be particularly challenging for some non-native English users.)

Little words are often a problem: they are easily skipped past visually as the brain fills in from context. Our digital tools can be especially tricky with little words; for instance, autocorrect often changes *in* to *on*, and vice versa. Errors may also appear in very familiar words (especially in phrases) simply because they *are* so familiar: the proofreader may mistakenly assume that such basic diction could not possibly be wrong, such as *and, with, the, some, does, like,* or *very*. I'm particularly bad for typing *your* instead of *you*, and a friend

of mine often swaps *now* for *know*. The writers you work with may also have predictable foibles that you can learn to anticipate.

Watch for word transpositions (e.g., *at every turn* versus *every at turn*). Transpositions are common in strings of short words and in changes made late in the process. Some experts suggest that speaking the words aloud slowly, with exaggerated articulation, will help you catch missing and misused language. When you're working slowly, you can mindfully process both the visual and the auditory information.

Commonly confused words

English contains hundreds of *homophones*: words that sound the same (or nearly the same) but are spelled differently and differ in meaning. Here's a short list of examples to get you thinking:

are	←→	our
ate	←→	eight
blue	←→	blew
canon	←→	cannon
forego	←→	forgo
heal	←→	heel
pail	←→	pale
plain	←→	plane
pole	←→	poll
sole	←→	soul
threw	←→	through
wail	←→	whale
wear	←→	where
which	←→	witch
vice	←→	vise

Homophones are a frequent source of sense issues in proofreading, particularly for people who proofread transcriptions (e.g., legal transcriptions, medical transcriptions). A typist may have transcribed a speaker's dictation or speech-recognition software may have done the work, but either way, human eyes need to check the document carefully for errors.

Listening and transcribing is challenging work, and listeners sometimes mishear words (e.g., *parity* heard as *parody*, *in essence* heard as *in a sense* or *innocence*, or *plaintiff* heard as *plaintive*). The only way to catch slips like this is with attentive proofreading that matches each word to its context. With practice, you'll learn many ways that words may be misspoken and misheard, and you'll gain greater ability to find and even anticipate errors. Turn this into an investment in yourself: when you fix an error, remember it. If you're keeping a personal running style sheet, note it there so you can recall this fix easily at some later date when it's relevant again.

Some words are confused because writers don't discern their usage or just make silly errors. Here's another list of examples to get you started.

As you invest in your skills and knowledge, you'll discover that you're catching more mistakes and working more efficiently.

adverse	⟷	averse
defuse	⟷	diffuse
disinterested	⟷	uninterested
enormity	⟷	enormousness
flaunt	⟷	flout
fulsome	⟷	full
gorilla	⟷	guerilla
have (or 've)	⟷	of
lustful	⟷	lusty
noisome	⟷	noisy
prescribed	⟷	proscribed
restful	⟷	restive

Again, the key is attentive proofreading. Keep your awareness of both spelling and meaning high. As you invest in your skills and knowledge, you'll discover that you're catching more mistakes and working more efficiently.

Numerous collections of commonly confused words have been compiled. See appendix 4 for a fuller list, check out the resources in appendix 5, or google "commonly confused words."

Proofreading alongside text-generation tools

More and more people are using voice texting and speech-recognition software as time-saving apps or to collect data and write reports on the go. These technologies are very good and getting better every year, but you must proofread the text generated by these tools *very* carefully. As the proofreader, you must both anticipate the errors these tools may produce and know how to correct them.

As I mentioned above, homophones are an issue with voice-to-text transcription. Thus, you must do one pass reading for sense, to ensure the words on the page are the intended words; then do another pass reading for consistency and correctness. Also note that spellings may differ according to the settings of the person using the software, which may not be your local settings. If you require Canadian spelling, for instance, use a resource like *Editing Canadian English* to support your process.

On smartphones, autocompletion and autocorrection can produce some spectacular errors. The range of mobile devices available, the software installed, and the keyboarding habits of individual users make generalizing about potential errors nearly impossible. Still, there are a few clues you can use if you're attempting to decipher a seemingly random string of words:

- With individual words, consider the adjacent keys carefully: *i* and *o* are common swaps, as are *r* with *t* and *a* with *s* (see figure 5.1). Just keep in mind that not only may the user have keyed the wrong letter, but also the device may

Figure 5.1 If you compare a standard keyboard and a mobile device's keyboard interface, it's easy to see how errors might occur.

have used that miskeyed letter as the basis for a word replacement.

- With phrases, you may need to assemble the letters into an anagram (which is, very simplistically, what the software has done). For example, my phone recently changed "big items" into "big times." It has also changed "of the" into the almost-anagram "often."

- Consider whether a small word may have been autocompleted or autocorrected into a different small word, such as *an/ and, ever/every, he/her, he/the, her/here, is/it, of/off, on/one, or/our, our/out,* or *the/they*.

- If a sentence breaks partway through, check whether the word or partial word before the period might have ended with *x, c, v, b,* or *n* — letters immediately above the space bar on most mobile keyboards. Devices sometimes perceive a "space" tap instead of one of these letters and insert a period, then start a new word.

- Autocorrection and predictive text can be sensitive to context but rely on probability to generate suggestions. Technical content that uses less-common words, phrases, and acronyms may contain errors introduced by the software's best guesses, for example, *PDF* (portable document format) versus *PFD* (personal flotation device), or *XLS*

(an Excel file extension) versus *XSL* (extensible stylesheet language).

- Most writers generate consistent slips — such as *cam* for *can* or *ya* for *us* — and the device learns the mistakes rapidly, so if you regularly work with the same writers, you'll soon grow skilled at deciphering their intentions.

If autocorrection and predictive texts are causing significant problems for writers you work with, remind the writers that these functions can be turned off. Writers can also reset the keyboard dictionary (where the software stores spellings the user has "taught" it) — a good idea if a writer is frequently fighting to override "learned" corrections. (Obviously, such scrupulous attention to correctness applies mainly in professional settings, not to personal communications.)

If you are proofreading on the fly — live-blogging, for instance, or posting data live on a broadcast — you need backup. Hand your phone or tablet to someone else and have that person calmly read your content word by word. Ask the person to read it aloud to you, exaggerating the pronunciation of each word; *listen carefully* to what you hear. If you're dealing with numbers, use COMPARISON PROOFREADING (see chapter 7), character by character, against the source. A confirmation process like this really doesn't take long — just a moment or two — and may save loads of embarrassment.

EXERCISE

Diction Issues

Choose the correct word for the context in each sentence below.

1. Kesha could not have anticipated the (affect / effect) of that evaluation on the employees' morale.

2. Based on the comments of the (disinterested / uninterested) evaluator, we should sell the portrait on the left.

3. The children had great fun (dying / dyeing) eggs.

4. The actor rushed off the stage in a fit of (peak / pique / peek).

5. Raisa has been a (principle / principal) actor in more than thirty shows but has rarely received the recognition she is due.

6. Sam makes (fewer / less) mistakes at school since her parents removed the TV from her bedroom.

7. Please (insure / ensure) you've followed the submission requirements for the assignment exactly.

8. Percy was puzzled about how to divide the cake (between / among) his five friends.

9. Beyoncé Knowles (lead / led) a resurgence of women's top-charting singles.

10. Fear that I might (lose / loose) the jewel made me reluctant to wear the necklace.

11. Lissa adores anyone (that / who / whom) thinks pancakes can be eaten for breakfast, lunch, or supper.

12. Emmet thought he would (forego / forgo) dessert that night.

13. This fall's collection offers looks you'll want to wear (everyday / every day).

Misspellings and minor mechanical problems are the major issue with text-recognition software (sometimes known as *optical character recognition* or OCR software), although today's software is more encompassing and more sophisticated than it once was. The software is often used to convert printed text to digital text when the original exists only on paper. The age and quality of the printing, the contrast between the ink and the paper, and the plainness or decorativeness of the source type may all affect how well the software operates and how many errors are introduced.

> **Although digital tools save time, accurate and logical text depends on human proofreading.**

Individual letters may be misread by the scanner. For instance, depending on the typeface, *i* and *I* may be misread as *l*, *a* may be misread as *s*, *g* may be misread as *q*, and *j* may be misread as *J* (and vice versa). Letters may also be misread as digits: *b* and *G* misread as *6*, *l* misread as *1*, *A* misread as *4*, and *O* misread as *0* (and vice versa). When certain letters are grouped together tightly, they may also be misread by the scanner; some common misreadings include *ri* as *n*, *fi* as *fl*, *fi* as *fr*, and *rn* and *ni* as *m* (and vice versa). (In a text I proofread recently, a character called Jumper sometimes showed up as Juniper because of the way the scanner interpreted the type.) Spell-checking will catch many of these errors if it is run — but it won't catch everything. Text-recognition software also frequently drops character formatting such as italics, boldface, subscript, and superscript, and may have trouble with diacritical marks (such as the accent on *crèche* or those on *Žižek*). These issues can be detected only by a proofreader's discerning eye.

If you are using text-recognition software with hand-printed or -written text, or OCR software with image-based PDFs, accuracy problems are much more frequent. Although text recognition is getting better in this area, human handwriting is idiosyncratic and scans can be imperfect. Both often deviate from the idealized models against which the software matches the letter forms it finds. Some software may learn common errors and users' habits over time, but when users are rushing or use specialized words and symbols, the likelihood of error increases. In these cases, you may need to compare the source copy against the machine-generated text or may need significant familiarity with the content to be able to discern errors and make appropriate corrections. Again, although digital tools save time, accurate and logical text depends on human proofreading.

And of course sometimes, despite all the technology and software available, people will choose to recreate text by keying it (or rekeying it) into a word-processing document. For some people this is a quicker solution than using a scanner or OCR software, but the quality of the resulting text depends on the keyboarder's skills, so careful proofreading — perhaps with a partner — is still required.

Something to keep in mind is that human tolerance for errors is generally fairly broad, but the context matters. A handful of proofreading errors in a book-length document probably won't cause much of a stir, but most readers will be quickly frustrated by errors in a short document. The publisher's status or authority — its relationship to its audience — also matters. Proofreading errors in an international magazine or an A-list scholarly journal are a bigger problem than in a community newsletter or a photocopied flyer. Proofreading errors in a technical context, where an order of magnitude could drastically affect the value of the information (think of a physician's dosing directions or an engineer's specifications as examples), are potentially dangerous, even life-threatening.

HOW TEXT-GENERATION TOOLS GET IT RIGHT AND WRONG

English syntax works in a logical, fairly predictable manner. When we begin speaking or writing a sentence, each word we select limits what can plausibly follow it. For example, once I write the word "my" to start a sentence, my choices are syntactically restricted to a noun (e.g., my *memory*), an adjective (e.g., my *happiest* ... a noun will to come next), or an adverb (my *very* ... an adjective will have to follow, and then a noun, e.g., *my very happiest memory*). Only certain parts of speech may follow the noun phrase, and so on.

A similar logic constrains English spelling. Once we choose a letter, only some letters can follow it. Because we recognize this logic (and because English users tend to write and speak using a fairly small set of words), programmers have been able to create routines that predict the most likely word to follow from one or two initial characters. Note that I said "most likely": humans are endlessly creative when we speak and write, and specific contexts may encourage us to reach for words outside the few thousand that make up most people's working vocabulary.

As such, predictive text and autocompletion (found on smartphones and in some word-processing setups) can be great tools, but they can also introduce unintentional errors. If you ever encountered the website Damn You Autocorrect, you likely remember (and perhaps cringe at) just how troublesome predictive text and autocorrect can be when we don't notice the "help" these tools have offered.

Numbers and math

As with proofreading names, assume that a number is wrong until you can confirm it is correct; if possible, check numbers against source copy. If the number has units, the same suspicion applies: there's considerable difference between 1 tsp and 1 tbsp of baking soda, or between nm for *nanometre* and nm for *nautical mile*. Be sure the unit makes sense in context, too (e.g., 10 m/h might be the right value in some settings, but 10 km/h makes much more sense in other settings).

Some consistent weak spots in copy involve numbers: dates, phone numbers, addresses, prices, and totals. Check these points carefully. Use a calendar, a directory, a calculator, or other resources to solve any problems, but always keep your role in mind. You are not fact checking, just confirming correctness and consistent treatment.

With phone numbers in particular, break the number into a pattern — for example, area code, three-digit string, four-digit string

— to confirm that each element is correct. Also ensure that the number refers to what it's supposed to refer to — that the toll-free number has a toll-free prefix, for example, or that a home phone number and a business number haven't been swapped.

When you are dealing with large amounts of numeric content, it may be necessary to compare your proofs against the source content. Partner proofreading — where one person reads the source text aloud to another person, who compares the content to the proof text — may be an appropriate strategy, particularly if the consequences for errors may be serious.

Beyond accuracy, keep in mind consistent treatment for numbers according to the assigned style guide (as discussed in chapter 1, pages 8–11; see also page 43). Be sure numbers are expressed as digits wherever they need to be read and compared easily: in data reporting, recipes, and technical processes, for example. Record the treatment of numbers (and their associated units, if necessary) on your style sheet.

Proofreading data

When you proofread data, numerical or otherwise, accuracy is, of course, paramount. Technical editing expert Carolyn D. Rude observes, "Because of the potential complexity of quantitative and technical material, which may contain many symbols and unusual type devices, the chances of errors occurring are greater than with paragraphs and sentences." Remember, numbers in particular represent facts, whether the number is an address, a statistic, a price, or a measurement. Check numbers character by character against a source text whenever possible, and think about the sense of the data you're examining in context. For instance, be sure percentages add up to 100 unless a note explains why they don't, and be sure graphic representations reflect numerical values (e.g., four and a half apples to represent a harvest of 4.5 tons). Be sure you understand why the dataset is presented the way it is so you can find any slips in the presentation logic.

Numerical information can be organized in many ways: according to magnitude, chronologically (to show trends through time), in rank order, or by other systems. Ensure related information is presented in consistent, comparable ways. The purpose of presenting numerical information is to support some larger message, not for the sake of the numbers themselves.

Much technical communication uses graphics in place of written text to illustrate patterns and relationships and to represent ideas at a glance. Typical graphics include tables, various forms of graphs, diagrams and illustrations, timetables, and flowcharts. Decisions about how best to present graphics are made long before proofreading occurs; the proofreader confirms that these elements display as intended and are correct, complete, consistent, and clear in their composition.

Check the ordering of items in tables, the scales on graphs, the slices in pie charts, the titles and element labelling on all figures, and any notes or legends that accompany the graphics. Gather together and confirm that all tables, charts, graphs, and other figures are referred to in the running text, depict what their captions describe, and are correctly numbered and sequenced. If the data have been reproduced or adapted from another source, the source must be correctly identified. If credit lines run with the graphics, ensure all credit lines are present (e.g., *Photograph by Kerry Matsu; used by permission*) or cross-check that the permission is stated elsewhere, if necessary. Because graphics are so condensed or so simplified, it is easy for the author to miss something that is obvious to the proofreader's fresh eyes. Query tactfully if the numbers don't add up, if a graphic seems incomplete, or if some aspect of the representation seems off.

Specialized materials

Proofreading specialized materials requires that you gather appropriate resources to support your work and that you work smart. If you need a specialized encyclopedia or dictionary, for instance, have it at hand. You may need a discipline-specific style guide, such as *Scientific Style and Format* (Council of Science Editors style) or *Canadian Guide to Uniform Legal Citation* (also known as the McGill Guide). If you proofread as a member of a team, ask team members for suggestions of resources to support your mutual work.

Next, think about process. Divide the task logically. What elements should you read side by side (e.g., tables beside other tables, captions beside other captions)? What material may need an extra pass by an independent set of eyes? Who is available to answer questions quickly if necessary?

A proofreader corrects things that are demonstrably wrong and queries everything else. You must trust that subject matter experts, writers, editors, and anyone else who might have been involved in earlier stages of document creation have corrected any factual errors and confirmed the accuracy of the technical content. Even if you are an expert in the subject area, if something doesn't pass your sniff test, query it rather than change it without checking. Proofreading is generally more effective when you're not deeply knowledgeable in the subject area, because you're more likely to notice a missing step or a procedure that doesn't entirely make sense. But remember your boundaries. It's rarely the

A proofreader corrects things that are demonstrably wrong and queries everything else.

proofreader's job to add in the missing step or recast cloudy prose. Simply point out your concern and work with the appropriate person or resource to resolve the issue.

In very high-stakes situations (e.g., where a genuine and serious risk exists for readers if the content is wrong, as in medical texts), documents should be reviewed by multiple proofreaders. Have several proofreaders found the same issues? Having both subject matter experts and non-experts reviewing the document can reveal lingering gremlins — as long as everyone understands and respects the ground rules of proofreading.

⫸ BUILDING A THOROUGH PROCESS

Proofreading for sense involves awareness, sensitivity, and anticipation, plus an openness to learning from your own and other people's mistakes. Listen to the document for intention, and ask questions when you truly need help. Some problems with sense cannot be resolved by the proofreader and must be queried. But many *can* be resolved — if the proofreader is attentive and thoughtful.

- Look out for words that have been transposed in a sentence or words that have been omitted from a sentence.
- Check for diction errors, especially homophones.
- When information follows an obvious pattern — such as alphabetical, numerical, or chronological order — ensure the pattern is followed consistently. If the text announces what is to follow — for instance, six points — ensure that is indeed what follows.

Proofreading machine-generated text can add an extra layer of challenge, as can working with data and technical content. The underlying process, however, remains the same: work slowly and methodically, simultaneously questioning everything and respecting the work that has already been done.

- Check the numbering of notes and figures; confirm that all figures, photographs, and illustrations are cross-referenced in the text unless they are strictly decorative.
- Confirm phone numbers and addresses, including email and website addresses.
- Check dates and times for consistent formatting as well as accuracy.
- Check units and currencies.
- If the document includes equations, formulas, or non-alphanumeric content, check these elements carefully against the source copy.
- Proofread with a partner when you work on documents generated by text-recognition or voice-to-text software.

WARMING UP TO PROOFREADING answer from page 57:
Note that 1998–2008 is a ten-year period, not a twenty-year period. Because the
time period is in a direct quotation, you'll need to query to know how to fix this
error.

✏️ **EXERCISE**

Chapter 5 Practice

Proofread this excerpt from a literary biography for overall correctness; for extra
practice, use correct markup symbols. Query any facts you find suspect.

Throughout her school years, Joasia's teachers fascinated and repelled her in equal measure. Even decades later she recalled the kindness of Mr. Eaton, her grade five teacher, who kept her after school one day - ostensibly for tutoring, to limit the potential ridicule of her peers — to talk about menstruation because Joasia's mother wasn't around to do it. What a conversation that must have been for a man in his late-twenties. And there was Mrs. Schmidt, the senior high science teacher whose confident manner and passion for learning inspired the entire class to achieve. And Orville Starchyk the history teacher who had his classes compose tableaux of important moments from Canadian history (with a generous helping hand from *Canada Vignettes* and other National Film Board documentaries). But then again there was Miss Richards, with her beehive hair and her whithering sarcasm, whose reading class was compose of owls, bluebirds, and starlings. Someone who should never have worked with children, never mind working-class kids from a small resource-based town. Ironically, Joasia was a starling that year.

Unquestionably, the teacher who made the greatest impression was Dr. Henrik Nicolas Diedrichs. Hailing from Toronto, Canada's glittering, capital city, with its live theatre and experimental publishers, its music scene and international design houses, he was glamorous, dazzling, almost star-like to his small-town students. Joasia's classmates from the period recall that Diedrichs loved his subject and made no bones about showing it. Indeed, he invited them to join him in performing scenes from Shakespeare, Ibsen, Brecht, inhibiting the lines with his body as well as his intellect. He brought poplar records to school and played them during class, turning off the lights and inviting students to move or draw or simply feel the lyrics and rhythms. He organized a debate club, a creative writing club, and a short-lived school newspaper. Young, colourful, and charismatic, Diedrichs was unlike anything the town had seen before.

Joasia was enchanted. Here at last was someone who shared her boundless enthusiasm for: words, poetry, line, and lyric; someone who didn't laugh when she earnestly explained the personalities and quirks and idiosyncracies of words; someone who suggested books and music and movies and ideas, which Joasia chased feverishly wherever the family made its semi-annual excursions to the big city. It was also from Diedrichs that Joasia absorbed the notion that literature was simply about living a full, emotional rich life. Yet it would be years before she could translate that understanding to the personal and begin creating, rather than being created by, literature.

Henrik Diedrichs's decision to move to Peace River, Alberta, in 1979 must be read against the larger back-to-the-land impetus then inspiring young people across North America. Having completed a doctrate in Canadian Literature (still an unusual focus at at the time) at the University of Toronto the previous year, Diedrichs felt alienate from the people and the land about which he had spent the last eight years studying. He was seeking an opportunity to live a simpler, more authentic life when he came across teh fateful advertisement for teaching jobs in remote communities. The Peace River School District was only too happy to accept his application and forwarded a salary advance of three thousand dollars to help defray the cost off his move.

6

Proofreading Visual Communication

Do you notice any errors in this graphic? *Answer on page 76.*

How the Arts Council's $50-million grants budget is distributed

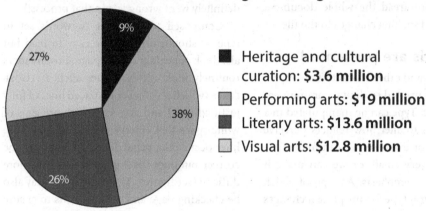

- Heritage and cultural curation: **$3.6 million**
- Performing arts: **$19 million**
- Literary arts: **$13.6 million**
- Visual arts: **$12.8 million**

Your job as proofreader will often include reviewing the visual elements of a document. You're not looking at the document merely as words: you're looking at the graphic presentation of the words, as well as the presentation of illustrative materials that accompany the words and the way the page is composed. Whether you receive them digitally or on paper, page proofs (sometimes called *galleys*) are designed and typeset and appear in near-final form. As proofreader, you ensure the pages both read correctly and look good.

Proofreading for visual consistency and correctness is sometimes called *production proofreading* because the proofreader is looking at elements of design and visual presentation that are added over the course of publication production. Here are some typical elements of page composition to consider:

- Consistent use of typefaces and type sizes throughout (in the body of the document and in smaller passages such as captions)
- Consistent margins, indentation, and alignment (also called JUSTIFICATION)
- Formatting and consistency of vertical lists
- Correct and consistent styling on block quotations

- Formatting and correctness of titles and subheads (various levels)
- Correctness and consistency of text accompanying figures and graphics
- Formatting and currency of running heads and footers (and their omission on pages that are intentionally blank)
- The presence of widows and orphans (very short lines left alone at the top or bottom of a column or page)

Most of the proofreader's communication about visual elements is done through queries. Remember your role as proofreader: even if you are the document's designer as well as its proofreader, proofread the whole document before you start making changes to the file.

How words are presented

Letters, words, and other characters are represented in most printed or digital communication using type. Type can be manipulated in a variety of ways to alter how readers perceive information. For example, we can make type very large or very small, or we can make it bold or italic for emphasis. As a proofreader, you are looking at type for any place it changes size, style, or colour unexpectedly. You must be able to examine how type is presented, to recognize when it deviates from specifications, and to mark it or know when to query it. This point is a matter of both correctness and consistency, but underlying it is a consideration for the eventual reader of the type. What will help or hinder the reader's understanding?

Anything that alters the ordinary perception of type makes it more difficult to proofread. The use of italics and boldface, for example, requires that the proofreader slow down, still reading character by character but also ensuring that the use of the italics/bold is appropriate in its context. Similarly, cursive fonts — typefaces that imitate handwriting — need extra attention. Cursive is normally used only in small passages, but those passages tend

to occur on documents people are likely to keep (e.g., wedding announcements and diplomas), so correctness really matters. Check character by character against source content, and query if anything seems suspicious.

Be similarly vigilant with headlines, title pages, posters, and ads — anywhere words have been formatted in short bursts with decorative, eye-catching fonts (usually called DISPLAY TYPE). Never assume these words are correct, even if they were correct before design. They may have been rekeyed or otherwise altered during the process. (As an example, I own a book whose front cover and full title page present the book's subtitle differently — something definitely went wrong late in that process.)

Composed text — that is, words set in type — should not only be easy to read but also look appealing on the page. Proofreaders routinely look out for issues such as LOOSE LINES (which are unevenly spaced lines of fully justified type) and RIVERS (which are gaps of white space that emerge when multiple loose lines occur on a page). The text itself may be correct, but poor spacing makes reading more difficult (see figure 6.1). Proofreaders may also be checking page and column ends to ensure columns/pages are symmetrical. Widows and orphans also make reading more difficult and make the page less attractive; proofreaders normally query widows and orphans.

If you read chapter 3 on punctuation and mechanics, you may remember some extended advice about hyphens there. When you're examining the visual presentation of text, hyphens need consideration again. Hyphens are inserted in words as they break across lines of text, and several typographic conventions have emerged to make hyphenated text easier to read and understand. Hyphenation can be turned off in layout software, but doing so can lead to other visual issues (such as a very ragged margin if the text is not fully justified and loose lines if it is). If the text is hyphenated, a few other issues can emerge. First, look out for

bad break — wrap up?

The underground press movement of the late 1960s, largely organized around protest movements such as the Civil Rights and anti-Vietnam movements, eventually brought forth hundreds of small feminist magazines and journals, including the (in)famous *Off Our Backs*, even a few in Canada. Most lasted only a few issues, often less than a year. Very few actual copies of many of these papers still exist. Some have been captured on microfilm in various libraries and archives.

Very tight line — adjust?

Loose lines — adjust? *bad break — wrap up?*

Some have been donated to various institutions as part of personal collections. Many, however, are today known only by their names and reputations. These publications were not necessarily sophisticated or even well manufactured. They were often produced in small runs, typed or even hand-written rather than typeset, and duplicated on mimeographs and photocopiers rather than with offset printing. Their immediacy and urgency, however, resonated with many people at the time.

stacked hyphens — adjust?

Figure 6.1 Some common issues with composed text are marked up in this example.

three or more consecutive lines ending with hyphens: these are called STACKED HYPHENS (see figure 6.1) and are considered an indicator of poor typography. Mark them and write a query for the layout staff. Some proofreaders also mark lines that end with a hyphen on a word that is already hyphenated (such as *anti-establish- / ment*). Finally, some proofreaders mark proper nouns (such as personal names, place names, and organization names) that break across a line or a page. When you're thinking about hyphens and other niceties of typography, always be guided by what you know about the intended readership of the document and how the document is likely to be used.

How words are supported

Once you've reviewed a document for typographic issues, it's time to look at other visual matters. Consider all illustrative materials and structural elements that help readers understand organization and hierarchy.

Examine every image. Beyond matching the image with its in-text description, check its placement. Images and figures should appear after they are discussed in the text (not before) and relatively close to that discussion. Then check the image quality. Is the image resolution sufficient — that is, are there enough pixels per inch — to display cleanly in the document's final format? Low-resolution images (75 to 100 ppi) are sufficient for onscreen display and office photocopying; much higher resolution — generally 300 ppi or higher for photographic images and 1200 ppi for line art and vector graphics — is usually required for DIGITAL PRINTING and OFFSET PRINTING.

While you're at it, ensure that photographs are laid in correctly and haven't been reversed or rotated in confusing or embarrassing ways. For example, if there are letters or numbers in the image, be sure they're right-reading (even if they're not truly legible). Problems with reversed images (called *flopped images* in publishing; see figures 6.2a, b, and c) can be difficult to detect if you're dealing with international content — for example, if a street scene is flopped so that any kanji characters on signage show up backwards, you might not recognize the issue unless you read Japanese. Similarly, rotated images in a technical context may not be as readily apparent to you as a non-specialist but may be obvious and troubling to an expert. If you can't confirm the orientation of an image, query it.

EXERCISE

Proofreading Style and Format

Proofread this table of contents from an anthology of perspectives about the writing life. Because you do not have a complete manuscript to refer to, make a list of the elements you would need to cross-check against the complete proofs.

Contents

One last point: ensure that images reflect the content under discussion. In July 2019, for example, a sharp-eyed reader noticed that the image supporting the headline "Black market weed prices have gone down since Canada legalized" on a popular blog was not of cannabis but of reindeer moss. Although the stakes in this case were fairly low, you can likely think of circumstances where including the wrong image could be more dangerous than funny.

Next, ensure captions and any required credit lines are present, accurate, and correctly formatted. The same advice applies to tables and graphs: check their titling and sequencing, cross-referencing, scale values (if appropriate), labelling, and overall correctness. Also be aware that the title and number generally run above a table but below a figure or a graph; disciplines may vary, however, so check the appropriate style guide as necessary.

Turning a printed document upside down can help to reveal issues with margins and gutters, with line ends, and with rivers of white space in fully justified text. You'll get a different view of the visual presentation, and problems may become much more obvious. Turning the document upside down may also reveal trapped white space, which occurs when a "shape" emerges between printed and unprinted areas on the page; this issue, however, may be beyond your authority as proofreader. If that's the case, point out the issue and leave it to the assigning editor to decide what to do. (In a high-profile ad or a book, such issues might matter enough to require fixing, but for most documents at this stage, likely not.)

Figure 6.2a When you proofread, look at images closely. Clues telling you that this image has been flopped include the way the models are holding their instruments, the way their tops are buttoned, and the flies on their pants.

Figure 6.2b This image makes sense visually until you look at the model's name tag.

Figure 6.2c A proofreader who does not know Arabic might not recognize that this image has been flopped. The image reads stronger with this flopped composition (that's why the designer flopped it), but creates an obvious error to anyone who can read Arabic or is familiar with Arabic stop signs.

In any place where words or letters are used graphically, such as on title pages and section markers, proofread the text carefully. Text used as a graphic represents a weak link in the production sequence, as the text may have been rekeyed by design staff, may not have been reviewed by an editor, and may be a comparatively new element in the layout. It is also easy to stop thinking of this sort of text *as* text, and therefore as something that needs to be proofread. Never assume text-based graphics are correct as presented (see figure 6.3).

If you're working with an extended text — text that runs more than a few pages — group the pages so that you can compare elements that are supposed to be similar. For instance, if you're proofreading a textbook, group all the chapter opening pages together and confirm that formatted elements have all been treated in the same or similar ways. Is the alignment

TWO TERMS TO KNOW

There are two abbreviations you should know when you're proofreading: FPO and TK. FPO stands for *for position only*. This abbreviation may overprint an image that is destined to be swapped for another image later in the production cycle. TK stands for *to come* (intentionally misspelled as an abbreviation) and generally appears in a space designated for an image or graphic that is not yet in place. Proofreaders should pay attention to either abbreviation, as proofreading is usually the last step before a document is printed, posted, or uploaded. Nothing at this stage should be TK, and very little should be FPO, so query these indications if you see them.

of the title consistent? Is the size of the title block consistent? Do all the chapters appear visually congruent?

Copy-fitting

Proofreading changes to text or layout sometimes cause the words in a document to exceed the space available. Designers can usually fix this problem using controls in the layout software, but at times the proofreader will be asked to cut words (never ideas) or rewrite sentences to make the text fit. This process is called *copy-fitting*.

Copy-fitting is uncommon but may be required when you must accommodate late changes. Do not undertake this work unless you have the authority to do so. If you must trim text, look for paragraphs that end with short lines: could you cut a few words in the paragraph so the short line is eliminated? Look for unnecessary modifiers, unnecessary repetitions, passive phrases that could be rewritten in active voice, and long words or phrases that could be expressed with single short words (e.g., *because* in place of *due to the fact that*), as long as the words aren't specific terms.

An issue related to copy-fitting is *dropped lines*, which occur when text overflows its space or is obscured by an image or graphic. A proofreader may recognize dropped lines because a page ends mid-sentence and does not continue on the following page or because the text at the top of a column or after a page turn reads as if something is missing. Write a query, marking where you suspect the issue occurred. You will need to proofread the text again once it is recovered.

GIBBON'S

The History of the Decline and Fall of
of the Roman Empire

Figure 6.3 Text used as a graphic may contain errors.

⫸ BUILDING A THOROUGH PROCESS

As you mark up any document, keep the design staff in mind. You must be able to communicate clearly to get what you need. I observed earlier that most designers and editors know standard markup, but remember that sometimes a face-to-face conversation is quicker and clearer than any amount of markup. Also remember that designers, like the writers and editors they support, are human and may make mistakes. This is one reason that closing the loop, which we'll discuss in chapter 7, is so important.

- Confirm that no elements are missing, all sections of the text are displaying as intended, and nothing has been added or deleted unintentionally.
- If your document includes interactive digital elements, test that links are live and correct, graphics are correctly embedded, and all components work as intended.
- Watch out for stray hard and soft returns (a hard return creates a paragraph break; a soft return forces a line end). These characters, usually imported invisibly from word-processing software, may create unexpected breaks in paragraphs and interrupt readers' flow.
- Check running heads/footers for consistent format, correct content, and correct spelling. (This content may not have been generated by the writer or reviewed by an editor.)
- Compare the table of contents to the body of the document for currency and accuracy. Check page numbers and titles to be sure they match.
- Check the chapter/section title area and subheads for correctness and formatting, especially if the document contains multiple levels of subhead.
- Follow cross-references, note markers, and page jumps to ensure their correctness.
- Review any change of typeface or type size: is it intentional?
- Watch line ends / new lines for repeated diction.
- Check the numbering or alphabetical ordering of vertical lists.
- Check dingbats (e.g., • or ✳) and punctuation on vertical lists. Font substitutions are a common problem with dingbats. Missing or inconsistent punctuation is also common on vertical lists (and style guides differ on their preferences for formatting such lists), so aim for consistency.

✏️ WARMING UP TO PROOFREADING answer from page 69:

There are math issues in this figure. The percentage values add up to 100, but the dollar values add up to only 49 million. Also, the relationship between the percentage values and the dollar values is incorrect for at least one of the numbers. Finally, a chart should indicate the source of its figures, although internal charts do not consistently do so. A proofreader must query all these issues.

EXERCISE

Chapter 6 Practice

Proofread the following post from an agriculture association's blog. Query any issues
with visual presentation. For extra practice, use correct markup symbols.

Let's Get Gardening!

Raspberries

One of the "must-haves" in many urban
gardens is a row of raspberries. Here are
a few basic facts about these delightful
plants and — more importantly — their
fruit.

Give your plants full sun and plenty of water.

History and Biology

The American red raspberry (*Rubus strigosus*) is native to large portions of Canada and the United States, primarily in or near boreal
forest. It is closely related to the Eurasian red raspberry (*R. idaeus*)
and for decades was thought of as a subspecies or variety of the Old
World plant. Today it is recognized as a distinct species. Most commercially grown plants derive from hybrids between these species.

Raspberries are complex perennials. The roots are perennial, the
canes (which are actually woody stems) are usually biannual. Roots
with first-year stems are generally planted in the spring as soon as
the soil can be worked. The following year the canes will flower and
bear fruit.

In Zone 3, raspberries are usually ready to pick in the third week of
July; the cans will continue to flower for a few weeks. Each raspberry
flower has five tiny white petals (in ornamental varieties the petals
are pink). Raspberry fruits are edible and tasty; raspberry leaves are
sometimes harvested for herbal teas.

Exercise continues on next page.

What they need

Raspberries grow best in full sun with regular water, although the
plants are tenacious and will grow
even in difficult conditions. To little
water will noticeably impair the height
of the canes and both the quantity
and quality of the fruit, so if the
summer is hot and dry, be prepared to water.

Numerous red varieties are available though greenhouses and
nurseries. Varieties may be classified according to when fruit is
produced (early, mid, or late summer) and the sweet/tart balance
of the berries. You may also find yellow varieties, which bare fruit
later in the season. These berries are delicious and tend to have a
honeyed flavour.

Reproduction

Raspberries reproduce primarily through
"suckers," the underground extensions of
a plant's main root system that yields new
above-ground stems a metre or two away
(three to six feet) from the original plant.
In a private garden, raspberry patches may
spread rapidly but need limited care other
than to remove dead canes and keep the
patch accessible enough for easy picking.
In a shared garden plot; however, you'll
need to be alert: suckering can be aggressive, and new stems may show up several
meters away from their "mother" plant. Use

*Caption goes here and describes
beautifuul rasperries.*

a garden knife to cut the sucker (you'll find it 15 to 25 cm (6 to 8
in.) below the surface) and remove the top growth.

Learn More!

For recipes, preserving tips, and directions to local U-Pick farms,
check out www.AbRaspberryGrowers.org.

7

Closing the Loop

Review the sentences below. Should you query any of them? Explain why you think so. *Answers on page 87.*

1. When we next see Obi-Wan, his light sabre is drawn.

2. Joanne and Kelly were married on November 31, 2018.

3. James Bond is famous for carrying a Walter PPK.

4. The dihydrogen monoxide warning is making the rounds on Facebook again.

At this point it should be clear that a proofreader is the person responsible for finding and marking errors in a document. There is, however, one further step we haven't discussed. The proofreader is not necessarily the person making the changes to the document (although in many settings the proofreader does this work, too). The proofreader, or someone working on the proofreader's behalf, must review the corrected document to confirm that the changes the proofreader called for have been made, that all queries have been addressed, and especially that no new errors have been introduced in the process. Check and check again. Only then is the proofreading complete. This crucial step, which I've called closing the loop, is the focus of this chapter.

Checking changes

Historically, proofreaders reviewed typeset pages against a marked-up copy of a manuscript to ensure the typeset pages matched the author's and the editor's intentions. This process was called COMPARISON PROOFREADING. Today it's rare to have reference copy to read against; rather, most proofreaders simply review the document in its almost-final form.

The process of comparison proofreading is still relevant, however, for checking rekeyed copy and for ensuring that all proofreading catches have been corrected and all queries addressed. This is done by comparing the current form of the document (the "live" copy) against the most recent set of changes (the "dead," or reference, copy).

The process is straightforward. After you mark up a set of changes, the changes (on paper or in a PDF) are sent to the appropriate person to be made on the master document. A new set of pages or a new PDF should be generated for the person closing the loop. If you're doing the work, you go through each change marked on the dead copy and confirm that it has been made on the live copy and no new errors have been created. (If a change has been made to a sentence, for example, re-read the entire sentence in case an agreement problem, a dropped word, or a transposition has emerged as a result.) If a change was missed or an error introduced, you mark it on the live copy and return the pages or PDF to the appropriate person. If you are the person making the changes, go through the complete proof before you start making changes: stay focussed so you don't miss any errors. (Paper markup may be easier to use at this stage, and for this reason some proofreaders, designers, and editors still prefer to proofread on paper.)

Examine dropped-in copy carefully, particularly when it has been dropped in at the last minute.

The process of generating new proofs and checking changes continues until everyone involved is satisfied that the document is clean and correct. Figure 7.1 represents how changes are normally checked. Regardless of whether you work on paper or onscreen, you must have both dead and live copies open side by side so you can check the changes methodically.

Sometimes when you are checking changes, you'll discover an error that was missed on earlier passes. That's okay! Mark it now and be glad you caught it. Then keep going. Don't let a single miss throw you; but if you find a large number of misses, consider proofreading (or having someone else proofread) the document again.

Boilerplate copy

BOILERPLATE COPY refers to generic text that is dropped into a document and customized as needed. It is common in legal and technical settings as well as in advocacy work and fundraising, where a standard form letter may be adapted slightly from year to year or campaign to campaign, and then personalized for each recipient, but otherwise remains unchanged.

Because it is used so freely and in so many contexts, boilerplate copy is often assumed to be correct when in fact it may contain errors — errors that were corrected on proofs in an earlier document without the corrections being transferred back to the boilerplate text itself. The lesson here is this: examine dropped-in copy carefully, particularly when it has been dropped in at the last minute. Never assume that you can skip proofreading it. When your proofreading job is finished, do what you can to ensure any faulty boilerplate text is corrected for future use.

A related problem may arise with documents that draw content from many sources, such as annual reports, grant applications, and database-driven web applications. Because of its diverse origins, such content may reflect a variety of standards and practices (for example, both Canadian and American spellings, variable spacing between numerals and units, and abbreviations with and without periods), yielding a highly inconsistent compiled document. If you are proofreading a document like this and have the time, it may be appropriate to do a light copyedit to regularize the styling and make the content more congruent. Then proofread the document as planned. If you are strictly proofreading, try to emphasize consistency. This will be slow work.

Late changes

A final weak link in the process is late copy, which refers to any text that has been added to the document after the document has been edited. Because it may not have been subjected to the same level of rigour, late copy may be

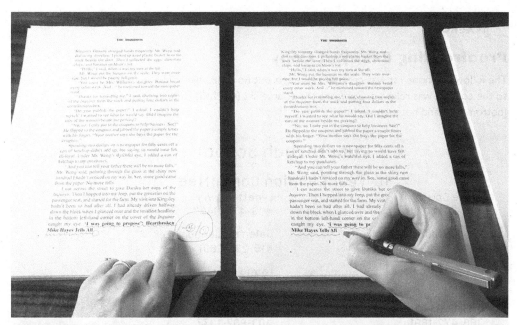

Figure 7.1 Proofreading changes on paper (top) are checked with the live (current) copy beside the dead (marked-up) copy. In a wholly digital workflow (bottom), many editors use dual monitors, one displaying the live copy, the other the dead copy.

EXERCISE

Proofreading Rekeyed Copy

The following phone list was created years ago, but no digital file could be found, so the content was rekeyed. Compare the source list (top half) to the rekeyed list (bottom half) and note any errors.

Kilbeth High School
10-Year Reunion Committee

Jaime Couch	403-362-7923	Lynette Lowry	403-475-5437
Kim Cushioner	614-476-9647	Galen Middendorf	416-220-8891
Brad Diedrichs	780-466-1982	Lainie Poon	250-251-1515
Nick Diemert	780-472-1891	Lisa Ramjohn	403-987-1377
Raquel Krisch	902-491-3662	Dena Sawa	306-949-3131
Geoff Lam	204-877-5204	Rae Suzanne	604-292-2555
Tanya Lee	519-522-2300	Harry Teacher	709-574-8412
Joycelyn Liska	604-778-5001	Steve Vesta	403-991-7711
Carrie Lothmar	250-918-1834	Tom Woodley	780-480-8007

Kilbeth High School
10-Year Reunion Committee

Jaime Couch	403-326-7923	Lynette Lowrie	403-475-5437
Jim Cushioner	614-476-9647	Galen Middendorf	416-220-8891
Brad Diedrich	780-466-1982	Lainie Poon	250-215-1515
Nick Diemert	780-472-1891	Lisa Ramjohn	403-987-1377
Raquel Krisch	902-491-3662	Dena Sawa	306-949-3131
Geoff Lam	204-877-5204	Raw Suzanne	604-292-2555
Tanya Lee	519-522-2200	Harry Teacher	709-574-8412
Jocyelyn Liska	604-778-5001	Steve Vesta	403-991-7771
Carrie Lothmar	250-918-1834	Tom Wooodley	780-408-8007

inconsistent or may contain errors of the kinds we've already discussed. If you know that a section of the document was added after the rest of the content was reviewed, give that section extra attention. You are, in effect, the first editor; your process is first a light copyedit and second the proofread you're undertaking. Be sure to refer to the project style sheet to ensure consistency.

A few final tips

Proofreading is not a game of Gotcha! As a proofreader, you are not trying to prove that the writers, editors, and designers you support are wrong or careless. Even the most conscientious writers and editors sometimes make mistakes or miss corrections — that's why proofreaders have a job to do. The role of the proofreader is to prevent writers, editors, publishers, and organizations from being embarrassed (or put in jeopardy) by the kinds of slips that all humans are prone to make.

Remember the ground rules from chapter 1? One of the rules says that successful proofreading requires *distance* — that is, mental space and emotional disengagement from

ADVICE FROM THE PROS

Here's some more advice from people who work with words and have to proofread regularly:

- "Here are a few things that I find need double-checking: Canadian spelling; titles and authors' names (because spell-check doesn't catch the aberrations); hyphens and dashes (which are sometimes confused) — also hyphenated words, since there don't seem to be any consistent rules for hyphenation; bad breaks at the ends of lines; agreement of verbs and pronouns with compound nouns; dangling participles; capitalization of the first word of a principal clause following a colon; and use of italics or quotation marks for titles." — Anne, scholar and editor

- "I'm terrible with *from/form*. Miss it all the time. *Councillor/counsellor* is one I fixed a lot at a magazine I worked for. And in the recipe column, I had to look out for *pantry/panty*." — Carmen, magazine editor

- "In the books I've worked on this year, it's mostly consistency issues. Canadian spellings, backwards apostrophes, consistent comma use, and consistency in number formatting are big ones that I look out for because I usually find issues." — Claire, book editor

- "Stuff I check and recheck: spelling — *judgement, bureau, it's* versus *its, accommodate, parallel* (double consonants in general, really). Other stuff: comma usage, consistency in bulleted lists, double spaces after periods, colon use, and hyphens versus en dashes versus em dashes." — Earl, business writer

- "Be positive and build trust with the writer. If the writer trusts you, it's much easier to have those conversations about what needs fixing. Have some fun and have a conversation with the writer. It should be a positive learning experience for both parties." — Garry, novelist

- "I would encourage all editors to a) read aloud, b) keep a list of any words/ phrases you have trouble with so you don't have to consult the dictionary every time you come across them, and c) when proofreading, use a guide of some kind, such as a ruler, to make sure you don't skip words or inadvertently read a word that isn't really there." — NJ, writer and editor

the text. This idea especially pertains when you must proofread anything you've written yourself: you must either have substantial distance from the document or ask someone else to review it for you. If you are the writer, editor, and proofreader, you must accept that sometimes an error will get past you. When that happens, do what you can to correct the error, then use it as a learning opportunity.

Almost every resource on proofreading emphasizes the idea of coming to the text with fresh eyes. There are a few reasons for this emphasis.

1. Human brains are pattern-discerning machines, evolved to make sense of stimuli quickly. When we have taken in enough information to make sense, we often stop attending — and if we're working with written text, that's when proofreading errors may slip through.

2. Humans are psychologically conditioned to perceive ourselves as congruent and correct, so it's difficult to see imperfections in our communications. After all, we know what we were thinking, what we intended to say — and that knowledge can mask a missing or misused word.

3. Most of us are under immense pressure to work quickly. Our world produces and consumes a great deal of information, often under punishing deadlines. Without a little distance from our own prose, it's easy to concede that copy is "good enough" without reviewing it rigorously (and sometimes "good enough" really *is* good enough). After all, in a 24/7 world dogged by short attention spans, a craving for instant gratification, and a fear of missing out, many people have learned to read around errors in prose, assuming quality must be compromised for speed.

But let me repeat a point I made earlier. When the stakes are very high — when the document you are proofreading absolutely must be correct and complete — you may need help. Asking a colleague to be a second — or third or fourth — set of eyes is not an admission of failure, nor is hiring a professional proofreader. Sometimes a job is too big or too important to do by yourself.

The basis of successful proofreading is planning. Before you actually put a pencil to the page (or a pointer tool to the PDF), take time to preview the text.

1. Identify the obvious problems.
2. Identify whether anything is still outstanding.
3. Identify the worst problem, the thing that *must* be fixed. Obviously, this is the issue to concentrate on. Consider any ripple effects that fixing this issue will have (e.g., if you delete a paragraph that causes several pages of text to reflow, the table of contents and/or the index may be affected). How will you manage them?

Don't skip this preview, even with a very short, simple document: the discipline of previewing will support you well when a deadline is tight. Widely respected editorial authority Wendalyn Nichols encourages you to evaluate a document on this basis: what you must fix, what you should fix, and what you could fix. If you must budget your time, think about your priorities and distribute your time and energy accordingly.

You have likely noticed that the emphasis throughout this book hasn't been on technology or SUBSTRATES (the surfaces to which print may be applied, e.g., paper, cardboard, or vinyl). The emphasis has been on getting you to think like a proofreader, regardless of the kinds of text you work with or the kind of workflow you follow. The goal of proofreading is to make effective, efficient catches. How a proofreader does so may vary from person to person, situation to situation. It's the end that matters, not the means.

As you become more experienced with proofreading, you'll notice that the process does not stand apart from writing and publishing but rather complements these processes in vital ways. To do the best work possible, a proofreader must understand the larger aim of the document: what it is for and how it intends its readers to respond. With that understanding in mind, the goal of enhancing the document's purpose should be the outlook that informs every change and query you make.

Close your door and put away your phone while you proofread.

A proofreading state of mind

The most effective proofreaders pay close attention to language at all times — even when they're not working. They notice patterns and exceptions to patterns, and they gather little nuggets of knowledge that help them detect and anticipate inconsistencies and errors. Your awareness of words — and in some cases your ability to play with words — will help when you're proofreading under time pressure.

The best proofreaders also possess self-awareness that helps them be effective. When during the day are you brightest and at your best? First thing in the morning? Between lunch and the end of the workday? In the evening, when you're on your own and the world is quiet? You should plan to proofread when you're most alert and your work setting is quiet. Distractions and interruptions make proofreading especially challenging, so close your door and put away your phone while you proofread.

Most proofreaders also cannot concentrate with the necessary intensity for more than a few hours, meaning that a proofreading job estimated to take twelve to fifteen hours may require three or four days to complete. Unless a document is very short and self-contained, you need to know your deadline and must manage your time so you're not rushing and so you have a chance to review the changes you've called for (if checking changes is within your purview). Allow time for breaks, so you can walk away and refresh your eyes. And if you find your attention wandering, *stop!* Put the job aside for a few minutes, or a few hours, until you're able to bring focus and energy to the task once more.

If you're proofreading a long document, be sure to make yourself comfortable while you work. Find a good source of light, work on a spacious surface, choose a comfortable seat, and plan regular breaks to keep your energy high and your eyes fresh.

We work in fast-paced, high-demand environments where mistakes can be embarrassing, costly, even dangerous. As a proofreader, you'll often be encouraged to race through your work — but don't give in to that pressure. Your first priorities are correctness and consistency, not quickness or volume. Always, *always* give yourself enough time for thorough proofreading: it may be the last step, but it is never the least.

▶BUILDING A THOROUGH PROCESS

Closing the loop is essential to completing a job with the care, quality, and overall professionalism we discussed at the beginning of this book. Not every proofreader is responsible for ensuring that marked-up errors have been correctly addressed and that queries have been answered, but if this task falls to you, take the time you need. There's no point in taking the process this far without seeing it all the way through.

- Clarify who is managing versions, making changes, and, if there are multiple proofreaders, consolidating changes. To support version management and avoid introducing late errors, there should be only one master "live" proof.
- Confirm that someone is responsible for checking that proofreading changes have been made.
- Check all captions for correctness and consistency: they may be late additions.
- Check and check again. Only after someone closes the loop is the proofreading complete.

The "slow" ethos — think Slow Food, Slow Fashion, Slow Scholarship — provides an excellent example for proofreading. Proofreading should be done slowly, calmly, and mindfully. What can you do to be the most successful proofreader possible? Here are a last few ideas that may help:

- Plan to work at your best time of day and limit distractions or interruptions.
- Work in a calm, quiet, well-lit setting whenever possible.
- To save time, bookmark pages you turn to often in your style guide.
- Note that errors tend to cluster. If you've just found an error, expect to find another one nearby.
- Recognize your foibles and compensate for them.
- Take regular breaks; pay attention to your concentration.
- Read aloud to yourself for an extra channel of information. Reading aloud also slows down your movement through the text.
- If you're interrupted while you're proofreading, mark your place and then restart a few lines above where you broke off. You'll get back in the groove more easily and catch anything that might have slipped through as your attention shifted.
- Extend your "proofreading state of mind" to those around you by framing proofreading as an aspect of organizational quality control.
- Don't sweat the truly small stuff. If you must perform editorial triage (setting priorities for what you must do versus what you *could* do — see page 5), invert Philip Pullman's observation quoted in chapter 2. That is, consider that if an issue won't be noticed by most readers, then your not fixing it also likely won't be noticed.
- Be patient and kind with yourself and with others working on the project.

⟨✏️⟩WARMING UP TO PROOFREADING answers from page 79:

1. You might query the spelling of *light sabre* (should be *lightsaber*, closed and with an -er).

2. Query November 31: does the writer mean November 30 or another month?

3. You might query the spelling of *Walter* (should be *Walther*).

4. You *might* query dihydrogen monoxide if you don't know this bit of satire: dihydrogen monoxide is another way of expressing the chemical formula for water, H_2O.

✍ EXERCISE

Chapter 7 Practice

Compare the dead and live copy shown below to be sure the corrections have all been made correctly. If not, mark up the live copy with the required change(s) for the next pass.

"Dead" Copy

Sunland Distilleries had already made a name for itself with its small-batch vodkas and a distinctive sage-infused gin. But back in 2017 André and Jean-Marc Gibeau decided to produce a line of crèmes. Little did they know this decision would generate one of the greatest technical challenges the distillery had faced to date and also unearth a long-misunderstood family secret. /a

A crème is a liqueur named for its key flavour. Crème de menthe, for instance, is boldly minty, crème de poire is pear-flavored, crème de mûre features blackberries and so on. The Gibeaus were inspired by their great-grandfather, Laurier Clément, an amateur vintner and cellar owner who was renowned in his tiny home-town of Vianne, France, for his crème de fraise des bois (wild strawberry liqueur) and crème de framboise (raspberry liqueur). /u

A crème lives or dies by the quality of the produce used in its making. Unlike wine, which is the product of the fermentation of grapes, the fruit or herb in a crème does not ferment. According to André, the fruit is crushed to release its organic compounds, stirred together with sugar — "A lot of sugar!" notes Jean-Marc — and then soaked with a neutral spirit, or carrier, for weeks or months. The fruit is then strained out and the resulting liqueur is bottled with little further processing. /è /n

Because the technique is so basic, there's just no way to mask poor-quality fruits. But securing a sufficient quantity of top-quality fruit in Lloydminster, Alberta, can be difficult. Fresh fruit begins to deteriorate within hours of picking, and today's long supply chains mean that unless the Gibeaus could find a local supplier, they would receive fruit a week or more after it had been picked — and that simply too long a wait for a delicate crème. (bad break) /ʒ /s

The challenge ramped up, however, when they opted to try their hands at crème de cassis. Crème de cassis, more prosaically known as black currant liqueur, is the crème of crèmes, in part because of the resurgent popularity of the Kir Royale cocktail, a luxurious blend of crème de cassis and Champagne. (close up) (lc)

Cheap crème de cassis, often produced outside of France with harsh spirits and fruit that has been macerated twice or even three times, bears a strong resemblance to lavender syrup, says local beer and wine consultant Margaux Kim. Extra sugar is used to mask the cheap fruit and shoddy processing, resulting in a liqueur that is almost sickeningly sweet, compromises any cocktail its used in and is undrinkable on its own. As a tribute to their great-grandfather, the brothers decided they would redeem this most storied of crèmes — with an Alberta flair. /ear /ℓ/⟿

"Live" Copy

Sunland Distilleries had already made a name for itself with its small-batch vodkas and a distinctive sage-infused gin. But back in 2017 André and Jean-Marc Gibeau decided to produce a line of crèmes. Little did they know this decision would generate one of the greatest technical challenges the distillery had faced to date and also unearth a long-misunderstood family secret.

A crème is a liqueur named for its key flavour. Crème de menthe, for instance, is boldly minty, crème de poire is pear-flavoured, crème de mûre features blackberries and so on. The Gibeaus were inspired by their great-grandfather, Laurier Clément, an amateur vintner and cellar owner who was renowned in his tiny hometown of Vianne, France, for his crème de fraise des bois (wild strawberry liqueur) and crème de framboise (raspberry liqueur).

A crème lives or dies by the quality of the produce used in its making. Unlike wine, which is the product of the fermentation of grapes, the fruit or herb in a crème does not ferment. According to André, the fruit is crushed to release its organic compounds, stirred together with sugar — "A lot of sugar!" notes Jean-Marc — and then soaked with a neutral spirit, or carrier, for weeks or months. The fruit is then strained out and the resulting liqueur is bottled with little further processing.

Because the technique is so basic, there's just no way to mask poor-quality fruits. But securing a sufficient quantity of top-quality fruit in Lloydminister, Alberta, can be difficult. Fresh fruit begins to deteriorate within hours of picking, and today's long supply chains mean that unless the Gibeaus could find a local supplier, they would receive fruit a week or more after it had been picked — and that's simply too long a wait for a delicate crème.

The challenge ramped up, however, when they opted to try their hands at crème de cassis. Crème de cassis, more prosaically known as black currant liqueur, is the crème of crèmes, in part because of the resurgent popularity of the Kir Royale cocktail, a luxurious blend of crème de cassis and champagne.

Cheap crème de cassis, often produced outside of France with harsh spirits and fruit that has been macerated twice or even three times, bears a strong resemblance to lavender syrup, says local beer and wine consultant Margaux Kim. Extra sugar is used to mask the cheap fruit and shoddy processing, resulting in a liqueur that is almost sickeningly sweet, compromises any cocktail it's used in, and is undrinkable on its own. As a tribute to their great-grandfather, the brothers decided they would redeem this most storied of crèmes — with an Alberta flair.

8

Putting Your Skills to the Test

Spelling Test

How good is your spelling of free-standing words? Go through the following lists and circle or underline any misspelled words.

1. intimidation truely sincerely mediocre rhubarb

2. refugia tragedy granddaughter sophmoric restaurant

3. politicking congradulations tyrannosaurus separate indivisible

4. descendents yacht weight Arctic curriculum

5. questionnaire contemptable sergeant parliament carburator

6. rhythmic vigilante alumnae connoisseur reccommendation

7. euphemistic nickle height caffeine dungeon

8. psychological personnal susceptible sociological Presbyterian

9. veterinary permittable individuel extraordinary despicable

10. desireable bankruptcy laboratory hygiene Caribbean

11. theorum registrar repentance Wendesday consciousness

12. cemetery deductable indict playwrite convalescent

13. arithmatic transcendent category scissors dutchess

EXERCISE

More Punctuation Practice

Punctuate and correct mechanics in the word groups below; query any other issues.

1. Omar asked his mentor she was nominated for a Governor Generals Award last year remember whether shed edit his manuscript

2. Taylor Swifts song Look What You Made Me Do which people seem to either love or hate broke several major records

3. Kimmy thought some other kids gave her the side eye and then laughed and she immediately worried was it the jeans

4. I cant remember where theyve put the ladies department since the last renovation but therere the shoes

5. I asked my students Have you read John Greens novel Turtles All the Way Down yet

6. This week we have specials on Thanksgiving and Halloween decor next weekend though were changing over to Christmas ornaments

7. Marvin the prime ministers office called youd better call back right now

8. Last year we were really lenient about admission averages this year however were going to have to be much more selective

9. Jenna Salisbury thought she couldnt miss on Broadway with her play Shakespeare Is the Absolute Worst

10. Minas phone number hasnt changed in years but her address changes regularly shes always looking for a cheaper apartment

11. This problem we should note certainly existed prior to Ricks arrival at the office and isnt his fault

12. Whered you think you put Jims hat last night in the fridge

13. In his poem A Valediction Forbidding Mourning Donne compares the strength of the lovers relationship to gold to airy thinness beat

✍ EXERCISE

Breaking Context

One of the most difficult things to do when we proofread is to read what's really there and not what we expect to find. I have deliberately keyed these sentences backwards to break their context. Check the sentences for errors. Query any other issues.

1. .erehpsomta on dah ecalp eht tub ,gnizama saw doof eht dias eH .noom eht no tnaruatser a ot tnew ecno dad yM

2. .tohs a ti evig to dediced eh keew tsal tub erofeb egnar nug a ot enog reven dah daD

3. .gniyortsed elos eb ot tuo denrut relcycer eohs a sa boj s'dad yM

4. .skcik rof tsuj rethar tub ti ta doog er'yeht esuaceb reccos yalp t'nod srehtaf tsoM

5. .yhsif elttil a was ti esuaceb ihsus eht diova I detseggus daD

6. .yad sih sekam yllaer tenalp the fo noitator eht em dlot ecno rehtaF

7. ''!htiw og ot ydob on evah yehT ?gnitaert ro kcirt etah snoteleks yhw wonk uoy oD'' ,dias daD

8. .dleif sti ni gnidnatstuo saw ti :renniw drawa na eb tsum worceracs ruo that dekramer daD

9. .nwod tup ot eblissopmi ti dnuof dna ytivarg-itna tuoba koob a daer ot dediced daD

10. ?repap tuoba ekoj elbaraet taht uoy llet dad ruoy diD

11. .yrotcafsitas ylno si stcudrop ercoidem sekam taht yrotcaf a syas dad s'daD

12. .ti gniod flesmih ees t'ndluoc eh esuaceb gniniart nam elbisivni pu evag rehtaf yM

13. .detsuahxe pu ekow dna srelffum tuoba demaerd dad ym thgin tsaL

EXERCISE

Proofreading a Recipe

Proofread the following recipe; query any issues you can't resolve on your own. For
extra practice, use correct markup symbols.

Delicious White Cake

1/2 cup canola oil
1/2 cup granulated sugar
1 egg
1/2 tsp vanilla
1/2 tsp almond extract
1 cup flour
1-1/2 tap bakinq powder
1/8 tap salt
3/8 cup milk

Grease and flour an 8-inch round cake pan. (Alternatively, pre-
pare a muffin pan with paper liners to make 12 cupcakes.)

Jn a medium bowl, beat together oil and sugar until mixture
is light and frothy. Add vanilla and almond extract; mix well until
thoroughly incorporated.

In a small bowl, sift together flour, baking powder, and salt.
Add to wet mixture in four potions, alternating with milk. Beat
mixture until smooth.

Pore batter into prepared pan. Bake cake 15 to 17 minutes
or until lightly golden-brown (13 to 15 minutes for cupcakes).
Remove cake from oven, cool slightly, then invent pan and cool
cake completely before icing.

EXERCISE

Proofreading Technical Language

Have you ever wondered who writes the copy for a shampoo bottle? Not only does someone have to write it; someone also has to proofread it, ingredients list and all. Proofread the label copy below; query any issues you can't resolve on your own. For extra practice, use correct markup symbols.

Natural Beauty
FLORAL HEALING SHAMPOO

Showoff what you've got! This soothing, smoothing formula cleans hair gently and leaves it strong and supple. No more snarls or tangles, just silky, shiny, beautiful hair. With its delicious bouquet of fruits and flowers to lift your spirits, Floral Healing Shampoo helps your hair live it's best day everyday.

Directions: Wet hair and apply a small amount of shampoo directly to hair and scalp. Lather, than rinse. For best results, apply Natural Beauty Floral Healing Conditioner after rinse.

Ingredients: Distilled water, soduim lauryl sulfate, cocamidopropyl betaine, sodium laureth sulfate, ethylene glycol distearate, propylene glycol, dimethicone cetyl alcohol, citric acid, panthenol, niacinamide, orchid extract, fruit extract, glucose, NaCl, sodium citrate, fragrence

♲ This bottle is recyclable where facilities permit

Learn more about this product and our company at www.noonaturalbeauty.co.uk

Imported by Noo Organoo Inc., Vancouver V6B 3P7

EXERCISE

Proofreading Organizational Communication

Proofread the following email message before it is sent to more than 1,200 staff members and organizational affiliates. Query any issues you can't resolve on your own. For extra practice, use correct markup symbols.

To: All_Users
Subject: Introduction of Vice President, Operations
From: uni-mail@CU.com
Date: August 14, 2023

As President and CEO of Cogs Unlimited, it is my great pleasure to announce that our hiring committees' search has been a success. Effective September 5, 2023, Alexa Sarnia, MBA will step into the role of Vice-President, Operations. As many of you will remember, Alexa was the Prairie Provinces Regional Manager form 2009 to 2015. Those of you with really long memories might know that Alexa started at the Cogs Unlimited locution in Brandon, Manitoba, as counter staff back in 1993!

In the Regional Manager's role, Alexa set a sterling example in many ways. She demonstrated efficient management of financial resources, developed new administrative structures and processes, initiated a market expansion into the Northwest Territories, and mentored managers and staff in 37 stores across his territory. Alexa exemplifies the kind of ingenuity and work ethic Cogs Unlimited seeks all senior employees. She hopes to inspire all CU employees to greater efficiencies and sales achievements.

I began this search in February 2023 with the assistance of C-Suite Management Consultants, who reached out through their international networks of executive partners to develope the broadest possible pool of candidates. Their outreach germinated more than 80 interested individuals. The hiring committee included managers from all regional offices, to ensure the incoming candidate would fit the CU culture. After developing a short list and conducting three rounds of interviews, we fund our new VP. I wish to acknowledge the members of the hiring committee who gave so generously of their time to make this hire happen.

Please join me in warmly welcoming Alexa back to Cogs Unlimited. I'm proud that she's part of our corporate family.

I.M. Grench
President and CEO
This account is not monitored for user replies.

✍ EXERCISE

Proofreading a Bibliography

Proofread the following bibliography; query anything you cannot verify for yourself. For extra practice, use correct markup symbols. The basic bibliographic format is as follows:

> Lastname, Firstname. *Title of the Work in Title Case*. Location: Publisher Name, year.

Bibliography

Anderson-Dargatz, Gail. *Race Against Time*. Victoria: Orca Book Publishers, 2016.

Atwood, Margaret. *The Burgess Shale: The Canadian Writing Landscape of the 1960s*. Edmonton: University of Alberta Press, 2017.

Biel, Joe. A People's Guide to Publishing: Build a Successful, Sustainable, Meaningful Book Business from teh Ground Up. Portland, OR: Microcosm Publishing, 2018.

Bowen, Gail. *Sleuth: On Writing Mysteries*. Regina: University of Regina Press, 2018.

Britt, Fanny. *Forever Truffle*. Toronto: Groundwood Books 2022.

Bright, Robin, *Sometimes Reading Is Hard*. Markham, ON: Pembroke Publshers, 2021.

Burch, C. Beth. *Grammar for Writers*. Bloomington, IN: Archway Publishing, 2017.

Dewar, Elaine. *The Handover*. Windsor, ON: Biblioasis, 2017.

Epp, Roger. *We Are All Treaty People*. Edmonton: University of Alberta Press, 2098.

Germano, William. *On Revision: The Only Writing That Counts*. Chicago and London: The University of Chicago Press, 2021

Grafton, Sue. *Y Is for Yesterday*. New York: G.P. Putnam's Sons, 2017. Green, John. *The Fault in Our Stars*. New York: Penguin Books, 2014.

Greenberg, Susan L. *Editors Talk about Editing*. New York: Peter Lang, 2015.

Harman, Eleanor, ed. *The Thesis and the Book: A Guide for First-Time Academic Authors*, 2nd ed. Toronto: University of Toronto Press, 2003.

Houston, Keith. *The Book: A Cover-to-Cover Exploration of the Most Powerful Object of Our Time*. Now York: W.W. Norton & Company, 2016.

Irvine, Dean, and Smaro Kamboureli, eds. *Editing as Cultural Practice in Canada*. Waterloo, ON: Wilfred Laurier University Press, 2016.

Johnston, Aviaq. *Those Who Run in the Sky*. Iqaluit, NU: Inhabit Media Inc., 2017.

Johnston, Wayne. *The Old Lost Land of Newfoundland: Family, Memory, Fiction, and Myth*. Edmonton: NeWest Press, 2009.

Juby, Susan. *The Fashion Committee*. Toronto: Penguin Teen, 2018.

King, Thomas. *The Inconvenient Indian: A Curious Account of Native People in North America*. Illlustrated edition. Toronto: Doubleday Canada, 2017.

Exercise continues on next page.

Koller, Katherine. *Art Lessons*. Winnipeg: Enfield and Wizenty, 2016.

Koupal, Nancy Tystad, ed. *Pioneer Girl Perspectives: Exploring Laura Ingalls Wilder*. Pierre, SD: South Dakota Historical Society Press, 2017.

Kowalski, William. *Epic Game*. Victoria: Orca Book Publishers, 2016.

Lemay, Shawna. "The Flower Can Always Be Changing." Windsor, ON: Palimpsest Press, 2018.

Leach, Sara. *Slug Days*. Toronto: Pajama Press, 2017.

Lorimer, Rowland. *Ultra Libris: Policy, technology, and the creative economy of book publishing in Canada*. Tornoto: ECW Press, 2012.

Mayr, Suzette. *Dr. Edith Vane and the Hares of Crawley Hall*. Toronto: Coach House Books, 2017.

McCue, Duncan. *Decolonizing Journalism: A Guide to Reporting in Indigenous Communitities*. Don Mills, ON: Oxford University Press, 2023.

McDonell, Terry. *The Accidental Life: An Editor's Notes on Writing and Writers*. New York: Knopf, 2016.

McLeod, Neal, *100 Days of Cree*. Regina: University of Regina Press, 2016.

Mount, Nick. *Arrival: The Story of CanLit*. Toronto: House of Anansi Press, 2017.

Ng, Celeste. *Little Fires Everywhere*. New York: Penguin, 2017.

Novik, Naomi. Uprooted. New York: Del Rey, 2016.

Peters, John Durham. *Speaking into the Air: A History of the Idea of Communication*. Chicago: University of Chicago Press, 2001.

Prescott, Tara. *Poetic Salvage: Reading Mina Loy*. Bucknell Univeristy Press, 2016.

Pullman, Philip. *The Book of Dust: La Belle Sauvage*. New York: Knopf Brooks for Young Readers, 2017.

Robinson, Eden. *The Sasquatch at Home: Traditional Protocols and Modern Storytelling*. Edmonton: University of Alberta, 2011.

Scalzi, John. *Don't Live for You Obituary*. Burton, MI: Subterranean Press, 2017.

Sileika, Antanas. *The Barefoot Bingo Caller*. Toronto: ECW Press, 2017.

Smart, Maya Payne. *Reading for Our Lives: A Literacy Action Plan form Birth to Six*. New York: Avery,2022.

Solnit, Rebecca. *Men Explain Things to Me*. Chicago: Haymarket Books, 2015.

Steeves, Andrew. *Sixty over Twenty*. Kentville, NS: Gaspereau Press, 2017.

Sword, Helen. *Air & Light & Time & Space: How Successful Academics Write*. Cambridge, MA: Harvard University Press, 2017.

Thomspon, Cheryl, and Miranda Campbell, eds. *Creative Industries in Canada*. Toronto and Vancouver: *Canadian Scholars*, 2022.

Weiner, Jennifer: *Hungry Heart: Adventures in Life, Love, and Writing*. New York: Washington Square Press, 2017,

Wohlleben, Peter. *The Hidden Life if Trees*. Vancouver: Greystone Books, 2016.

Zevin, Gabrielle. *Young Jane Young*. Chapel Hill, NC: Algonquin Books, 2018.

EXERCISE

Proofreading a Resumé

A resumé is a high-stakes form of communication that requires flawless proofreading. Ensure there are no mistakes in the following document. For extra practice, use correct markup symbols.

Alice P. Liddell

Seeking a position in communications and community engagement where I can share and enhance my award-winning creativity and analytical skills

555 Rabbit Hole Road
Didsbury, Alberta T0M 0W0
(403) 780-5555
APL@freemail.ca

Queen of Hearts Baked Goods, Calgary, Alberta
Manager, Communications and Marketing

KEY ACCOMPLISHMENTS
- Lead a fledging company to local and regional customer brand recognition through creative, energetic communication strategies
- Recognized by the Baking Association of Canada with gold medal awards in 2014 and 2017 for Industrial Content Marketing

DUTIES
- Solely responsible for planning, implementing, and evaluating communications and branding strategies for an industrial bakery with clients across Western Canada
- Writing and editing content and responding to followers across multiple social media channels
- Writing and editing website content, including twice-weekly blog posts
- Writing copy and developing visual concepts for print collateral including signage, posters, catalogues, flyers, and mailers
- Handling news releases, maintaining an up-to-date media contact list, and handling information and interview requests from media
- Special event planning

Alberta Theatre and Stage Network
Communications and Marketing Coordinator

- Writing and editing website copy
- Writing and editing a biweekly digital newsletter for more than 900 recipients across western Canada (members and general pubic)
- Writing and designing print and digital marketing materials to promote ATSN events and members shows
- Preparing grant proposals for operational and project funding

---

Regina University College Press
Marketing Assistant

- Wrote website copy and maintaining title information on website
- Developed media contacts database
- Wrote or co-wrote catalogue descriptions for forthcoming titles
- Assisted with event planning and author relationships

Education

Global Standard Certification (ongoing
  International Association of Business
  Communicators Academy

BA (English Literature)
  Regina University College
High School Diploma (Honours)
  J.A. Fife High School, Olds

References available upon request

EXERCISE

Proofreading a Social Media Timeline

Proofread the following series of social media posts from a municipal development's communications unit. Assume any facts are accurate; correct only language issues. For extra practice, use correct markup symbols.

Ambrose Village

The riverside community that's anything but flat! Join our smart green development by the Saskatchewan River.

 Ambrose Village @AmbroseVillageYXE Sep 2

Happy Labour Day! Our Business Office is closed this weekend, but be sure to check out our newest show home on Cavanaugh Road. #showhome #VillageLiving

---

 Ambrose Village @AmbroseVillageYXE Aug 23

Its back to school next week. Looking for a welcoming community with a K–8 school your kids can walk to? Check out Seesequasis School at the heart of Ambrose Village. #families #schooldays #AutumnIsComing

---

 Ambrose Village @AmbroseVillageYXE Aug 13

It sure is hot! Don't forget your refillable water bottle. Wear a hat that shades your face. Keep kids and pets out of hot vehicles. Tomorrow's prediction: more of the same! #YXEWX #weather #hot

---

 Ambrose Village @AmbroseVillageYXE Aug 2

Looking for something to do this long weekend? Go for a stroll in beautiful Tomson Park at the centre of Ambrose Village. Follow Yurkiw Road from 1st Street. The kids will love our play ground!

#families #play #summer

 Ambrose Village @AmbroseVillageYXE Jul 17

Guests visiting Saskatoon this summer? Keep them cool at the YWCA pool, just one block from the northeast corner of Ambrose Village. Check out a map here: tiny.url/4321 #swimming #summer #VillageLiving

---

 Ambrose Village @AmbroseVillageYXE Jul 8

Join CKXM Radio at our show homes on Bowen Blvd this Saturday, July 13, 1 to 4 pm. Giveaways, music, plus enter to win $10,000 dollars toward the purchase of you new home in Ambrose Village.

#prizes #showhome #VillageLiving

Ambrose Village @AmbroseVillageYXE Jul 1

Happy Canada Day, everyone! Join our street party on Bury Road between 1st and 4th. Face painting, snacks, family fun. Fireworks at 11:00 pm! #celebrate #Canada #summer

Ambrose Village @AmbroseVillageYXE Jun 25

Until the end of July, you can save up to $28,000 on a new home in Ambrose Village Phase 5. Drop by one of our show homes or visit www.AmbroseVillageYXE.ca for more details.

Ambrose Village @AmbroseVillageYXE Jun 18

Are you ready for The Saskatchewan Jazz Festival? Running June 22 to 29, it's a bonanza of music, musicians, and fun. Several of the venues are just steps form Ambrose Village. #jazz #music #FunIsHere

Ambrose Village @AmbroseVillageYXE Jun 3

This is the month of the Strawberry Moon, according to Indigenous tradition. Maybe you should plant some strawberries in your new home garden! #VillageLiving #gardening #sweet

Ambrose Village @AmbroseVillageYXE May 20

Happy Victoria Day! The business office is closed for the long weekend, but check our out show home parade along Cavanaugh Road. #showhome #VillageLiving #celebrate #summer

Ambrose Village @AmbroseVillageYXE May 15

Just a reminder that with the spring weather, the streets around Tomson playground will be busier. Please watch your speed and keep out community safe! #kids #safety #VillageLiving

Ambrose Village @AmbroseVillageYXE May 12

We wish mothers everywhere a cheerful and loving Mother's Day. And to our own moms, hello and thanks, with lots of love. #celebrate #moms

Answer Keys

1. Jebediah was principal floutist of the Winnipeg Amateur   / a
   Philharmonic Society.

2. A recent pole suggests photocopier rage is an issue for   / L
   millions of Canadians.

3. The education ministers outrageous conduct made further   / ᵛ
   discussion impossible.

4. Myrtle put her hand/over the centipede protectively.   / ✎

5. Oscar Wilde wrote, "But Nature is so uncomfortable. Grass is
   hard and lumpy and dump and full of dreadful black insects."   / a

6. Her laughter at that moment seemed unbarably cruel.   / e

7. The mink farm was on the outskirts off town.   / ✎

8. Giving you year-end bonus to a charitable organization will   / r
   feel great.

9. What makes certain pants of speech so important?   / r

10. The cupcakes that were siting on the counter had disappeared.   / t

11. It is the solemnity of the ritual that make it so compelling for   / s
    believers.

12. The Muggles had not been warned about werewolf lurking in   / the
    the area.

13. Samson Golong brought irrefutable incidence of political   / ts
    interference to the attention of the police.

CHAPTER 1 PRACTICE (PAGES 20–21)

The Modernism Appreciators Guild

14 Baez Street

New York, New York

10017 USA

Re: Maria Alicia Ipanema

To the members of the residency committee:

I have known Maria Alicia Ipanema for more than ten years. She was my student in an

English composition course when she was completing her diploma in library technology, and

almost a decade later, I was her supervisor as she competed her MA in Modernist Literature. / 1

In these capacities, I have come to know Ms. Ipanema well: have advised her on various

matters, read her writing in a variety of genres, and watched her talent develop. She has

stayed in touch with me since her graduation and continues to mature as a creative writer.

For this reason I believe Ms. Ipanema would be an excellent candidate for a residency at the

Modernism Appreciators Guide.   / 1d

From my observation of Ms. Ipanema in class and while she was completing her

master's thesis, I feel she has both the need to work in solitude and the practical skills to get

along successfully with others in a retreat setting. Ms. Ipanema is intelligent but also wise, / g

compassionate, and resilient. She is ready to find a wider creative community; given the

chance, she will become an important literary voice. She simply need an opportunity.   / s

As the recipient of a scholarship from the University of Timmins and a bursary from the Manitoba Board of Culture and the Arts, Maria Alicia Ipanema has already been recognized locally and regionally for her talent and skill. I hope the Modernism Appreciators Guild, too, will be able to boast of Ms. Ipanema's successes, acheived with the Guild's support. ⒷⓇ

Ms. Ipanema currently works as a professional communicator, and I'm sure you recognize the cost such work can exact from a creative soul. A residency providing both peer support and dedicated time to write, reflect, and dream will allow this talented woman to purse her artistic goals and advance in her craft. Her knowledge of libraries and librarianship /u complements her writing skill and makes her an ideal fit with the opportunities available from the Guild.

Should you need any additional information about Maria Alicia Ipanema, please do not hesitate to contact me at (705) 555-9995. Thank you for considering this most deserving applicant.

Yours sincerely,

Joelle Lloyd-Ali, PhD

Chair, Graduate Studies

Department of Literature and Comparative Studies

University of Timmins

EXERCISE: THINKING ABOUT SPELLING (PAGE 24)

Below I've listed the preferred spellings according to the *Canadian Oxford Dictionary*, 2nd edition. Your dictionary might provide different spellings. Note that spelling practice is not uniform across Canada. Editors and writers do vary; at a minimum, spelling should be consistent within a single document.

focusing

curb

wont [ensure the intended word isn't *won't* or *want*]

omelette

aging

traveller

realize

light bulb

appendices *or* appendixes [Your choice of "appendices" versus "appendixes" may depend on context. Are you referring to a bodily organ or a point in a text?]

villain

encyclopedia

glamorous

co-operative

fulfillment

humorous

auxiliary [ensure the intended word isn't *axillary*]

enrolment

fetus

practised

accommodate

adrenalin

defence

storey

paycheque

plow

yogourt

jewellery

mochaccino

shovelled

manoeuvre

EXERCISE: IDENTIFYING WORDS OF CONCERN (PAGE 26)

What you circle may vary depending on your confidence with spelling, but at a minimum you should be examining the proper nouns (personal names). You might also have wanted to check the words *transcend*, *pre-reading*, and *complement*, and may have given some thought to hyphenation and various compounds (such as *award-winning*).

EXERCISE: PROOFREADING SPELLING (PAGE 27)

My spell-checker caught most of the errors in these sentences, but missed a few. Remember that you may not have access to a spell-checker when you're proofreading a document.

1. My granny's house was littered with dust-catching <u>collectibles</u> and <u>mementos</u>. [Note that my spell-checker considers "collectables" correct, but the dictionaries I consulted do not.]

2. We were genuinely <u>surprised</u> when Dr. Fuhr took the job as departmental <u>liaison</u> officer, but he's sure to excel in that role.

3. Melinda's on-air pronunciation was crisp, but her <u>changeable</u> accent was a distinct liability.

4. The politician <u>publicly</u> disavowed common vices like smoking and drinking, but partook of them regularly in private.

5. People's <u>curiosity</u> about Jen's <u>tattoos</u> makes her uncomfortable.

6. Summer <u>temperatures</u> sound so much cooler when expressed in <u>Celsius</u> degrees, don't they?

7. Have the investigators reached a <u>consensus</u> about whether a recurrence represents a <u>tendency</u> or a trend?

8. Such <u>minuscule</u> differences barely register without sophisticated equipment to weigh and measure the pullets day by day. [Note that the spelling "miniscule" is hotly contested and some dictionaries now include it as a variant of the preferred *minuscule*.]

9. The representation of party events as news led to questions about <u>propaganda</u> and generated sharp <u>resistance</u> at the annual policy convention. [Note that *led* (the past tense of *to lead*) is frequently misspelled as "lead"; watch for this error.]

10. So <u>basically</u> we are stuck evaluating whether he <u>acquired</u> the substances accidentally or deliberately. [Note the correct spelling of accidentally — it follows the pattern of *basically*, not *publicly*.]

11. The tedium of Bert's relationship was punctuated by increasingly rare moments of <u>ecstasy</u>.

12. There is, of course, no problem with an <u>occasional</u> argument, but escalating unresolved conflict can lead to a relationship breakdown.

13. The table at the back just ordered two mojitos, two <u>daiquiris</u>, and a pitcher of sangria, plus a <u>margherita</u> pizza.

CHAPTER 2 PRACTICE (PAGES 31–32)

Note that "Island" takes an initial capital throughout, based on local usage. If you have a project style sheet, this is the kind of detail to record on it.

Vancouver Island Summer Guide

There's no need to leave home for fun. The Island's many festivals, cultural happenings and seasonal celebrations will keep you busy all summer long!

JUNE

Port Alice: Founders' Days
(rom) / *JUNE 1–2*
This colorful community celebration brings /u residents home year after year. Live music, traditional arts and crafts sale and a duck derby for the kids. Don't miss the fireworks Saturday night, followed by a pancake breakfast Sunday morning.

Campbell River: Sea Do
JUNE 14–16
A celebration of the bounty of the Strait of Georgia. Love entertainment, food / i truck alley, boat show, logging skills demonstration and a dedicated kids' / r activity centre. Community dance Saturday evening and fireworks Sunday at midnight!

Port Renfrew: Solstice Celebration
JUNE 20–23
The Island's only sun-worship festival! Music, dancing, arts, food and family-friendly fun. Interpretive shore walks daily on the hour between 10 a.m. and 4 p.m. Be sure to sing up for the sandcastle *(br)*

competition!  ⟨? wrap orphan to previous column?⟩

Nanaimo: Toy Sailboat Regatta
JUNE 29–30
The world's biggest toy sailboat regatta! Gather on Newcastle Island for food, fun and hourly competitions. Onshore / ⌐ events include boat building for kids and educational displays on sailing, boat safety and green boating.

JULY

Sidney: Kids' Festival of Reading
JULY 2–12
The Beacon Avenue bookstores transform into an extravagant alley of book-related fun. Highlights include a Harry Potter-themed party (July 5) and *Where* / ⌐ *the Wild Things Are* night (July 8), plus author readings and book giveaways at participating stores.

Port MacNeill: Legends of Logging
JULY 6–7
Do you have what it takes to become a legend of logging? Logging-related sports *(br)* and displays of brute strength are the focus of Port MacNeill's annual take on the Highland Games. Spectator or competitor, all are welcome. This year we have food / d trucks!

July 10 date OK re July 12-21?

Port Alberni: History Fest

12–21 JULY *(tr)*

Celebrate the Alberni Valley's long history of fishing, forestry, farming and good living. Catch the history parade downtown Saturday, July 10, and don't miss the Indigenous education events (various locations). Enjoy a slice of our living history!

Tofino: Ocean Blues Fest

JULY 19–21

Not in its tenth year, the Ocean Blues */10th*
Fest is one of Canada's best-kept secrets. This year's lineup includes Chicago Blues Reunion, MonkeyJunk, Ry Cooder, Colin James and the David Wilcox Experience, plus */d*
a dozen new legends-in-the-making.

Port Hardy: End of the Isle Music Festival

JULY 25–28

A family-friendly festival featuring Alex Cuba, Michael Franti, Captain Tractor and many local favorites. Now at a new location */u*
with lots of space for oceanside camping — or catch the shuttle from the downtown hotels. Onsite food and merch tables.

AUGUST

Parksville: Twilit EDM Festival

AUGUST 1–4

Non-stop music and light shows beginning Thursday evening, plus food vendors, arts and crafts tables and daytime beach events. Come for a day or the weekend! Admission restricted to those 19 and older.

Sidney: Beach Feast

AUGUST 3–5

50 / More than fifty food trucks, representing
everything from street food to fine
dinning, will make their way to Sidney for

the August long weekend. Trucks will be serving from 11 a.m. to 2 p.m. and from 5 to 9 p.m. each day. Bring you appetite! */r*

Cowichan Bay: Bacchanalia

AUGUST 9–11

An adults-only celebration of wine and winemaking. Sample wines from across the Island and around British Columbia. Daily talks about wine appreciation, cooking */o*
with wine, wine vacations and wine */ ـ*
collecting. Featuring local food plus live music! *(tr)*

Telegraph Cove: Killer Whale Week of Welcome

AUGUST 4 TO 10 */ Y~*

Located directly across the Broughton Archipelago from Blackfish Sound, Telegraph Cove is the place to celebrate the start of the salmon run and the return *(lc)*
of the resident Orcas. Education events, *(lc)*
boat tours, art exhibitions and more! */ ـ*

Ladysmith: Quietus

AUGUST 17–18

Shhh! This is a gathering especially for introverts. Features large spaces with comfortable seating for you to bring a book and read silently with others. Quite *(tr)*
dining in dim-lit venues. Watch for book sales and themed sales tables (various locations).

Chemainus: Mini-Bard Festival

AUGUST 25–SEPTEMBER 2

A theatre festival for everyone, the Mini-Bard Festival presents dramatic readings and cut-down versions of some of Shakespeare's best-loved plays. You haven't */s*
experienced Shakespeare until you've seen the seven-minute Hamlet! *(ital)*

EXERCISE: PRACTISE PUNCTUATING (PAGE 39)

Here are my solutions; in some cases, you could make different choices. (Incidentally, both the spell-checker and the grammar checker on my word-processing software picked up only a small number of these errors.)

1. What Professor Snape, the meanest teacher in the school, did next was unbelievable.

2. Siobhan watched the knife-throwing contest interestedly; after all, her father had been an expert with knives.

3. Imogen concluded that day-to-day operations shouldn't be negatively affected by last month's shutdown.

4. "Then it's off to jail with you, Nefario!" the superhero announced triumphantly.

5. No wonder it's so cold in here! The thermostat's on the weekday setting.

6. Stacy enjoyed the antics of the scotch-drinking pirates at Jack's Bar last night.

7. The professor asked her class, "What could you do to improve your composition process?"

8. My colleague dislikes yelling at his students: he'd rather stare at them until they settle down.

9. Jonson wondered why the dogs had been barking in the compound yesterday.

10. As it turns out, however, Prufrock doesn't have the strength to force the moment to its crisis.

11. "You have to ensure your vehicle is securely stored whenever you're away!" the site manager shouted.

12. We'd learned several good money-saving tips in Gail's column the previous day.

13. The panel featured three women: Emma Jeela, best known for her work as a showrunner; Kamilla Tong, a leading footwear designer; and Janelle Marchand, an award-winning sculptor and philanthropist.

EXERCISE: PLURAL VERSUS POSSESSIVE (PAGE 40)

1. dress's

2. Oilers

3. tights

4. people's

5. scissors'

6. coaches' [There are two teams, so there are two coaches making the decision. The noun *coach* needs to be made plural to *coaches* before it is made possessive with an apostrophe.]

7. country's

8. children's

9. others'

10. grandparents

11. family's

12. circuses

13. Bennets'

EXERCISE: CAPITALIZATION (PAGE 42)

Here is the letter with conventional capitalization in place.

Attn: Amanda Bedelya

Sosevere Social Sciences and Humanities Publishing
909 East Queen Elizabeth Parkway
Toronto, ON M5W 2N1

Re: Dissertation Royalties

Please find enclosed two copies of a form that was sent to me last week. The form pertained to me but is addressed to someone else's name at my home address. In the past Sosevere has sent small royalty payments to me at this address using my correct name, and I suspect an error has been introduced into your system. My letter is intended to correct that error.

Although the enclosed forms bear the name "Beatrice Quimby," they should be made out to "Wilhemina Fosse." My dissertation, *The Essential Made Concrete in the Poetry of Robert Kroetsch*, was defended in the Department of English, Faculty of Arts, at the University of Edmonton in 2010. The address on Havitur Way in Shackleton, Saskatchewan, is the only one you should have on file for me, as it is my permanent home address and has been for more than a decade.

Again, in the past, Sosevere has correctly issued small payments to me with respect to my dissertation's use. In 2018, however, I submitted a Revenue Canada tax disclosure form at Sosevere's request, and I suspect there was a processing error with that form that has led to the misidentification on the forms I have enclosed. Since the sum involved this year appears to be zero dollars and zero cents, there is presumably little urgency to this correction, but for the sake of records and my continued academic publishing, I need to know that this error has been corrected.

I look forward to receiving your written confirmation that the correction has been made; in the meantime, I have retained one copy of your form in case I need it.

If you should need to reach me directly, please call me at 306-555-9090. Thank you for your prompt attention to this matter.

Sincerely,

Dr. Wilhemina Fosse
Associate Professor
Department of English
University of Saskatoon
c/o 123 Havitur Way
Shackleton, SK S0S 0N0

CHAPTER 3 PRACTICE (PAGE 47)

Dada Arthur

Arthur Cravan, born Fabian Avenari- ⌃, / us Lloyd on May 22, 1887⌃ was a wholly original Modernist. A nephew of Oscar Wilde, he aggressively rejected conventional society. He travelled widely as a young man, throughout ⌐/ Europe⌐ and across America, making his way by picking up odd jobs and boxing. He is best remembered today as the pugilistic forefather of the Dada movement who once said, "Let me state once and for all: I do (tr) not wish to be civilized⌃."

One of Cravan's many proto-Dadaist exploits involved preparing a French-language magazine (*Maintenant* — "Now") of his work in his (close up) own hand⌐writing and selling it on the streets of Paris from a wheelbarrow. He published ⑤ issues, made up (sp) entirely of his own writing plus illus-(tr) trations from various French artists. He delivered a lecture at a learned society that he opened by firing a pistol into the air. He then ~~preceed~~- proceeded / ed to make provocative statements about art, culture, and life, then concluded by throwing his briefcase ⌐/ at the apparently ⌐rapt audience. ⌐/ Perhaps⌐ his most outrageous performance involved his offer to kill himself in front of an audience to placate those who were offended by his taunting and criticism. The event was scheduled for a local bar; Cravan promised to lecture in a jock strap (to please the ladies, *bien sûr*) and drink ⌐Absinthe as he per- (lc) ished. But when the crowds — and the reporters — showed up, Cravan harangued the public for their tawdry tastes (how gauche to show up for a suicide!), then gave a high-ly⌐conventional presentation about /⌐ French writer⌐ Victor Hugo. /⌐

Mina Loy met Arthur Crav⌐n in /a New York in April 1917, and they were instantly attracted to each other. They were married less than a year after meeting. The couple spent the early part of 1918 bumming across Mexico, desperately poor but also fiercely in love. By July Mina was pregnant, and the couple decided to return to Europe.

They had to⌐ little money to travel /o together, so Mina sailed to Buenos A⌐res to wait for Arthur, who was to (tr) follow a few days later. But Arthur disappeared and was never heard from again⌃ he was presumed lost at /; sea. Arthur's disappearance marked a crucial turn in Loy's life.

EXERCISE: SUBJECT AND VERB AGREEMENT (PAGE 50)

1. selects   8. was

2. were   9. are

3. present   10. has

4. sits   11. was

5. does   12. is

6. reminds   13. has

7. are

EXERCISE: MODIFIERS (PAGE 52)

Here are my corrections to the sentences; you may have come up with something slightly different, but your solution should be similar. In the notes that follow each correction, I've identified what's wrong with the original sentence.

1. Moving here, there, and everywhere, I had no constants in my life but my family and my painting. [The original sentence contains a DANGLING MODIFIER.]

2. Elmer feels bad about running into you with his bike. [The original sentence reflects confusion between adjective and adverb.]

3. The silverskin should be left intact when you cook ribs on the barbecue. [The original sentence contains a dangling modifier.]

4. While I was running to catch the LRT, my phone fell out of my pocket. [The original sentence contains a dangling modifier.]

5. The kicker moved the ball barely seven yards. [The original sentence contains a MISPLACED MODIFIER.]

6. When one is starting work as an apprentice meat cutter, the expectations may be confusing and the hours long. [The original sentence contains a dangling modifier.]

7. This perfume, even under its generic, off-label copy name, would smell just as sweet. [The original sentence reflects confusion about the need for an adjective to complement a linking verb.]

8. When the product is used as directed, allergic reactions are rare. [The original sentence contains a dangling modifier.]

9. For a lot of people, this was a devastating fire that did not need to occur. [The original sentence contains a misplaced modifier.]

10. We enjoyed a really tasty sundae at the diner the other day. [The original sentence reflects confusion between adjective and adverb.]

11. After I saw Arthur I decided I would never smoke again. — or — I decided I would never smoke again after I saw Arthur. — or — I decided after I saw Arthur that I would never smoke again. — or — I decided that after I saw Arthur I would never smoke again. [The original sentence contains a specific instance of misplaced modifier often called a "squinting" modifier because it could apply to either clause. In a case like this, where several corrections are possible, choose the "best" solution based on the sentences that come before and after the sentence requiring correction.]

12. A portion of the proceeds from the sale of this book will go to the University Music Department and a memorial fund for victims of Hurricane Maria. [The original sentence contains a misplaced modifier.]

13. After today, this behaviour is absolutely and without question going to stop. — or — After today, this behaviour is going to stop, absolutely and without question. [The original sentence contains a specific instance of misplaced modifier often called a split infinitive. Most editors will let unobtrusive split infinitives go, but usually change awkward ones like this — this is a matter of judgement.]

CHAPTER 4 PRACTICE (PAGE 55)

There is *so* much potentially wrong here. The key is not to invest too much time in an ephemeral document. Yes, the grammar is a bit wobbly, but does it prevent readers from understanding and acting?

We're Looking To Score With You! /lc /lc

Portage la Prairie Womens Floor Hockey League / ˇ

Have you wanted to play floor hockey since leaving school? We do too!
Join us every Thursdays for a fun "beer league" experience! / ℟

Thursdays, 8:45 to 9:55 p.m. /⊙

(please arrive at least 5 minutes early and / be
changed and ready to play—there are locker rooms on site)

close up

Sept 6 - Dec 20 and Jan 3 –May 30 /$\frac{1}{N}$ /$\frac{1}{N}$

Portage Community Sportsplex, 30 Dauphin Drive

$20 per drop-in (cash only) or $550 for the whole season /⊙

No experience necessary /⊙

Bring your own plastic stick (available from (Cdn) Tire). / Canadian
Pucks and pinnies provided.

For more information please call or text

Sara Lamiroden @ **204-555-1212**.

Women only, 19+ /⊙

EXERCISE: TRAINING YOUR ATTENTION (PAGE 58)

1. There are structural problems with the novel, notably some repetition and several saggy passages ~~in the novel~~. [Omit the redundant phrasing.]

2. For professional communicators, **libel** — a lasting form of defamation — is an ever-present risk.

3. Beware of one editorial foible: editors want everything to be right and tend to stress **needlessly** about insignificant copy.

4. In British Columbia, prosecutors are referred to as Crown **counsel**. [If you don't live in British Columbia, this usage may not be familiar. Be prepared to check phrasing like this to ensure a spelling error doesn't become an error in fact.]

5. Hormones increase or **inhibit** how quickly cells perform their ordinary functions.

6. We are alarmed to learn that the person in question has developed still more disruptive behavioural **tics** over the past year.

7. Most breeders for the ornamental plant industry, worth some $40 billion globally, simply ignore the **fragrance** of flowers, preferring instead to focus on high-value qualities like colour and vitality.

8. Lately it's rare to read a business story and not discover some **marquee** organization announcing layoffs or an earnings downgrade.

9. The **word** *tattoo* derives from a Tahitian word, *tatu*, meaning "to mark something."

10. The first blacksmiths in Lower Fort Garry were English, imported specifically by the **Hudson's** Bay Company. [This is a tricky point of knowledge: a geographic name (Hudson Bay) versus a corporate name (Hudson's Bay). As you become more experienced with proofreading, slips like this are less likely to get past you.]

11. Everyone was embarrassed at discovering the couple in the **throes** of passion.

12. Always review your writing carefully to check whether you have **forgotten** any words. [You could also use any other logical verb here, such as *omitted, missed,* or *skipped*.]

13. His grandfather had put up thirty pounds for third-class passage to Canada on the Norddeutscher Lloyd liner *Prinz Heinrich*. [Trick question! There are no errors in this sentence, but do note the words that deserve special attention.]

EXERCISE: DICTION ISSUES (PAGE 62)

1. effect
2. disinterested
3. dyeing
4. pique
5. principal
6. fewer
7. ensure
8. among
9. led
10. lose
11. who
12. forgo
13. every day

CHAPTER 5 PRACTICE (PAGE 67)

Throughout her school years, Joasia's teachers fascinated and repelled her in equal measure. Even decades later she recalled the kindness of Mr. Eaton, her grade five teacher, ‖/who kept her after school one day — ostensibly for tutoring, to limit the potential ridicule of her peers — to talk about menstruation because Joasia's mother wasn't around to do it. What a conversation that must have been ๑/for a man in his late twenties. And there was Mrs. Schmidt, the senior high science teacher whose confident manner and passion for learning inspired the entire class to achieve. ⌐/And Orville Starchyk the history teacher who had his classes compose tableaux of important moments from Canadian history (with a generous helping hand from *Canada Vignettes* and other National Film Board documentaries). But then again there was Miss Richards, ⌒/with her beehive hair and her whithering d/sarcasm, whose reading class was compose of owls, bluebirds, and starlings. Someone who should never have worked with children, never mind working-class kids from a small resource-based town. Ironically, Joasia was a starling that year.

Unquestionably, the teacher who made the greatest impression was Dr. Henrik Nicolas Diedrichs. Hailing from (Toronto,) Canada's ⊘ ๑/glittering capital city, with its live theatre and experimental publishers, its music scene and international design houses, he was glamorous, dazzling, almost star-like to his small-town students. Joasia's classmates from the period recall that Diedrichs loved his subject and made no bones about showing it. Indeed, he invited them to join him in performing scenes from Shakespeare, Ibsen, Brecht, ina/ hibiting the lines with his body as well as his u/ intellect. He brought poplar records to school

⊘ check: Toronto is not the capital of Canada

and played them during class, turning off the lights and inviting students to move or draw or simply feel the lyrics and rhythms. He organized a debate club, a creative writing club, and a short-lived school newspaper. Young, colourful, and charismatic, Diedrichs was unlike anything the town had seen before.

Joasia was enchanted. Here at last was someone who shared her boundless enthusiasm for words, poetry, line, and lyric; someone/๑ who didn't laugh when she earnestly explained the personalities and quirks and idiosyncrasies /s of words; someone who suggested books and music and movies and ideas, which Joasia chased feverishly wherever the family made its /ก semi-annual excursions to the big city. It was also from Diedrichs that Joasia absorbed the notion that literature was simply about living a full, emotional rich life. Yet it would be years /ly before she could translate that understanding to the personal and begin creating, rather than being created by, literature.

Henrik Diedrichs's decision to move to Peace River, Alberta, in 1979 must be read against the larger back-to-the-land impetus then inspiring young people across North America. Having completed a doctrate in /o Canadian Literature (still an unusual focus at/ⓚ at the time) at the University of Toronto the/๑ previous year, Diedrichs felt alienate from the /d people and the land about which he had spent the last eight years studying. He was seeking an opportunity to live a simpler, more authentic life when he came across the fateful adver- ⓑ tisement for teaching jobs in remote communities. The Peace River School District was only too happy to accept his application and forwarded a salary advance of three thousand dollars to help defray the cost of his move. /๑

EXERCISE: PROOFREADING STYLE AND FORMAT (PAGES 72–73)

The elements you would need to cross-check against the complete proofs are the section titles, the chapter titles, all authors' names, and the starting page numbers of all chapters and front/back matter elements.

Contents

Should this be 174?

THE STATE OF THE AUTHOR

should there be a page reference here?

These page numbers seem to be in boldface — they shouldn't be. Please check.

CHAPTER 6 PRACTICE (PAGES 77–78)

Let's Get Gardening!

Raspberries

One of the "must-haves" in many urban gardens is a row of raspberries. Here are a few basic facts about these delightful plants and — more importantly — their fruit.

Give your plants full sun and plenty of water. ⟨?⟩

History and Biology

The American red raspberry (*Rubus strigosus*) is native to large portions of Canada and the United States, primarily in or near boreal forest. It is closely related to the Eurasian red raspberry (*R. idaeus*) and for decades was thought of as a subspecies or variety of the Old World plant. Today it is recognized as a distinct species. Most commercially grown plants derive from hybrids between these species.

⌐Raspberries are complex perennials. The roots are perennial; the ~~/;~~ canes (which are actually woody stems) are usually ~~biannual~~. Roots /biennial with first-year stems are generally planted in the spring as soon as the soil can be worked. The following year the canes will flower and bear fruit.

In Zone 3, raspberries are usually ready to pick in the third week of July; the cans will continue to flower for a few weeks. Each raspberry /e flower has five tiny white petals (in ornamental varieties the petals are pink). Raspberry fruits are edible and tasty; raspberry leaves are sometimes harvested for herbal teas.

(left align, not fully justified)

⟨?⟩ Is this the right caption? I don't think so; I think it works better with the second image. Replace the current caption with something like "Who doesn't love delicious raspberries?" ?

What they need /(caps)

[margin note: image should align with first line of text]

[margin note: text very close to image — OK?]

Raspberries grow best in full sun with regular water, although the plants are tenacious and will grow even in difficult conditions. To little /o water will noticeably impair the height of the canes and both the quantity and quality of the fruit, so if the summer is hot and dry, be prepared to water.

[note: ? Use caption from first image here?]

Numerous red varieties are available though greenhouses and /r nurseries. Varieties may be classified according to when fruit is produced (early, mid, or late summer) and the sweet/tart balance of the berries. You may also find yellow varieties, which bare fruit /ear later in the season. These berries are delicious and tend to have a honeyed flavour.

Reproduction

Raspberries reproduce primarily through "suckers," the underground extensions of a plant's main root system that yields new /ʃ above-ground stems a metre or two away 3/6/ (three to six feet) from the original plant. /ft. In a private garden, raspberry patches may spread rapidly but need limited care other than to remove dead canes and keep the patch accessible enough for easy picking. In a shared garden plot, however, you'll /; need to be alert: suckering can be aggressive, and new stems may show up several /tr meters away from their "mother" plant. Use /wrap up/ a garden knife to cut the sucker (you'll find it 15 to 25 cm (6 to 8 /? in.) below the surface) and remove the top growth.

Caption goes here and describes beautifuul rasperries. ?

[note: These values don't agree — which are correct?]

Learn More!

For recipes, preserving tips, and directions to local U-Pick farms, /lc check out www.AbRaspberryGrowers.org.

[note: Replace caption. How about "Raspberries don't require much care beyond pruning and managing suckers."?]

EXERCISE: PROOFREADING REKEYED COPY (PAGE 82)

Kilbeth High School
10-Year Reunion Committee

Jaime Couch 403-362-7923	Lynette Lowry 403-475-5437
Kim Cushioner 614-476-9647	Galen Middendorf 416-220-8891
Brad Diedrichs 780-466-1982	Lainie Poon 250-251-1515
Nick Diemert 780-472-1891	Lisa Ramjohn 403-987-1377
Raquel Krisch 902-491-3662	Dena Sawa 306-949-3131
Geoff Lam 204-877-5204	Rae Suzanne 604-292-2555
Tanya Lee 519-522-2300	Harry Teacher 709-574-8412
Joycelyn Liska 604-778-5001	Steve Vesta 403-991-7711
Carrie Lothmar 250-918-1834	Tom Woodley 780-480-8007

Kilbeth High School
10-Year Reunion Committee

Jaime Couch	403-32⁄4-7923 (tr)	Lynette Lowrie	403-475-5437 /y
Jim Cushioner	614-476-9647 / K	Galen Middendorf	416-220-8891
Brad Diedrich∧	780-466-1982 /s	Lainie Poon	250-2⁄15-1515 (tr)
Nick Diemert	780-472-1891	Lisa Ramjohn	403-987-1377
Raquel Krisch	902-491-3662	Dena Sawa	306-949-3131
Geoff Lam	204-877-5204	Rae Suzanne	604-292-2555 /e
Tanya Lee	519-522-2⁄700 /3	Harry Teacher	709-574-8412
(?) Joycelyn Liska	604-778-5001 (tr)	Steve Vesta	403-991-77⁄71 /1
Carrie Lothmar	250-918-1834	C/Tom Woodley	780-4⁄08-8007 (tr)

I see that this is the spelling on the source document but please confirm it is correct

CHAPTER 7 PRACTICE (PAGE 88–89)

Sunland Distilleries had already made a name for itself with its small-batch vodkas and a distinctive sage-infused gin. But back in 2017 André and Jean-Marc Gibeau decided to produce a line of crèmes. Little did they know this decision would generate one of the greatest technical challenges the distillery had faced to date and also unearth a long-misunderstood family secret.

A crème is a liqueur named for its key flavour. Crème de menthe, for instance, is boldly minty, crème de poire is pear-flavoured, crème de mûre features blackberries and so on. The Gibeaus were inspired by their great-grandfather, Laurier Clément, an amateur vintner and cellar owner who was renowned in his tiny home-town of Vianne, France, for his crème de fraise des bois (wild strawberry liqueur) and crème de framboise (raspberry liqueur).

A crème lives or dies by the quality of the produce used in its making. Unlike wine, which is the product of the fermentation of grapes, the fruit or herb in a crème does not ferment. According to André, the fruit is crushed to release its organic compounds, stirred together with sugar — "A lot of sugar!" notes Jean-Marc — and then soaked with a neutral spirit, or carrier, for weeks or months. The fruit is then strained out and the resulting liqueur is bottled with little further processing.

Because the technique is so basic, there's just no way to mask poor-quality fruits. But securing a sufficient quantity of top-quality fruit in Lloydminster, Alberta, can be difficult. Fresh fruit begins to deteriorate within hours of picking, and today's long supply chains mean that unless the Gibeaus could find a local supplier, they would receive fruit a week or more after it had been picked — and that's simply too long a wait for a delicate crème.

The challenge ramped up, however, when they opted to try their hands at crème de cassis. Crème de cassis, more prosaically known as black currant liqueur, is the crème of crèmes, in part because of the resurgent popularity of the Kir Royale cocktail, a luxurious blend of crème de cassis and champagne.

Cheap crème de cassis, often produced outside of France with harsh spirits and fruit that has been macerated twice or even three times, bears a strong resemblance to lavender syrup, says local beer and wine consultant Margaux Kim. Extra sugar is used to mask the cheap fruit and shoddy processing, resulting in a liqueur that is almost sickeningly sweet, compromises any cocktail it's used in and is undrinkable on its own. As a tribute to their great-grandfather, the brothers decided they would redeem this most storied of crèmes — with an Alberta flair.

EXERCISE: SPELLING TEST (PAGE 91)

Here are the misspelled words.

1. truely [truly]

2. sophmoric [sophomoric]

3. congradulations [congratulations]

4. descendents [descendants]

5. contemptable [contemptible], carburator [carburetor]

6. reccommendation [recommendation]

7. nickle [nickel]

8. personnal [personal or personnel]

9. individuel [individual]

10. desireable [desirable]

11. theorum [theorem], Wendesday [Wednesday]

12. deductable [deductible], playwrite [playwright]

13. arithmatic [arithmetic], dutchess [duchess]

EXERCISE: MORE PUNCTUATION PRACTICE (PAGE 92)

Here are my solutions; in some cases, you could make different choices.

1. Omar asked his mentor — she was nominated for a Governor General's Award last year, remember? — whether she'd edit his manuscript.

2. Taylor Swift's song "Look What You Made Me Do," which people seem to either love or hate, broke several major records.

3. Kimmy thought some other kids gave her the side eye and then laughed, and she immediately worried: was it the jeans?

4. I can't remember where they've put the ladies' department since the last renovation, but there're the shoes.

5. I asked my students, "Have you read John Green's novel *Turtles All the Way Down* yet?"

6. This week we have specials on Thanksgiving and Halloween decor; next weekend, though, we're changing over to Christmas ornaments.

7. Marvin, the prime minister's office called; you'd better call back right now.

8. Last year we were really lenient about admission averages; this year, however, we're going to have to be much more selective.

9. Jenna Salisbury thought she couldn't miss on Broadway with her play *Shakespeare Is the Absolute Worst*.

10. Mina's phone number hasn't changed in years, but her address changes regularly: she's always looking for a cheaper apartment.

11. This problem, we should note, certainly existed prior to Rick's arrival at the office and isn't his fault.

12. Where'd you think you put Jim's hat last night — in the fridge?

13. In his poem "A Valediction: Forbidding Mourning," Donne compares the strength of the lovers' relationship to "gold to airy thinness beat."

EXERCISE: BREAKING CONTEXT (PAGE 93)

Note that some sentences contain no errors — and that they're all dad jokes!

1. .erehpsomta on dah ecalp eht tub ,gnizama saw doof eht dias eH .noom eht no tnaruatser a ot tnew ecno dad yM

2. .tohs a ti evig **ot** dediced eh keew tsal tub erofeb egnar nug a ot enog reven dah daD

3. .gniyortsed elos eb ot tuo denrut relcycer eohs a sa boj s'dad yM

4. .skcik rof tsuj **rehtar** tub ti ta doog er'yeht esuaceb reccos yalp t'nod srehtaf tsoM

5. .yhsif elttil a **saw** ti esuaceb ihsus eht diova I detseggus daD

6. .yad sih sekam yllaer tenalp **eht** fo noitator eht em dlot ecno rehtaF

7. "!htiw og ot ydob on evah yehT ?gnitaert ro kcirt etah snoteleks yhw wonk uoy oD" ,dias daD

8. .dleif sti ni gnidnatstuo saw ti :renniw drawa na eb tsum worceracs ruo **taht** dekramer daD

9. .nwod tup ot **elbissopmi** ti dnuof dna ytivarg-itna tuoba koob a daer ot dediced daD

10. ?repap tuoba ekoj elbaraet taht uoy llet dad ruoy diD

11. .yrotcafsitas ylno si **stcudorp** ercoidem sekam taht yrotcaf a syas dad s'daD

12. .ti gniod flesmih ees t'ndluoc eh **esuaceb** gniniart nam elbisivni pu evag rehtaf yM

13. .detsuahxe pu ekow dna srelffum tuoba demaerd dad ym thgin tsaL

EXERCISE: PROOFREADING A RECIPE (PAGE 94)

Delicious White Cake

 (?1)

1/2 cup canola oil
1/2 cup granulated sugar
1 egg
1/2 tsp vanilla
1/2 tsp almond extract
1 cup flour
1-1/2 tap baking powder /s
1/8 tap salt /s
3/8 cup milk

(?2) Grease and flour an 8-inch round cake pan. (Alternatively, pre-
pare a muffin pan with paper liners to make 12 cupcakes.)
I / In a medium bowl, beat together oil and sugar until mixture
is light and frothy. Add vanilla and almond extract; mix well until
thoroughly incorporated. (?3)
   In a small bowl, sift together flour, baking powder, and salt.
Add to wet mixture in four potions, alternating with milk. Beat /r
mixture until smooth.
ur / Pore batter into prepared pan. Bake cake 15 to 17 minutes
or until lightly golden-brown (13 to 15 minutes for cupcakes).
Remove cake from oven, cool slightly, then invert pan and cool /r
cake completely before icing. (?4)

(?1) Is this a low-resolution image? Replace?

(?2) Missing "preheat oven" direction? To what temperature?

(?3) The egg does not appear in the method. Should the
     sentence read "Add egg, vanilla, and almond extract"?

(?4) Should there be a recipe for icing, too?

EXERCISE: PROOFREADING TECHNICAL LANGUAGE (PAGE 95)

Natural Beauty
FLORAL HEALING SHAMPOO

Showoff what you've got! This soothing, smoothing formula cleans hair gently and leaves it strong and supple. No more snarls or tangles, just silky, shiny, beautiful hair. With its delicious bouquet of fruits and flowers to lift your spirits, Floral Healing Shampoo helps your hair live it's best day everyday.

Directions: Wet hair and apply a small amount of shampoo directly to hair and scalp. Lather, than rinse. For best results, apply Natural Beauty Floral Healing Conditioner after rinse.

Ingredients: Distilled water, sodium lauryl sulfate, cocamidopropyl betaine, sodium laureth sulfate, ethylene glycol distearate, propylene glycol, dimethicone cetyl alcohol, citric acid, panthenol, niacinamide, orchid extract, fruit extract, glucose, NaCl, sodium citrate, fragrence

This bottle is recyclable where facilities permit

Learn more about this product and our company at www.noonaturalbeauty.co.uk

Imported by Noo Organoo Inc., Vancouver V6B 3P7

EXERCISE: PROOFREADING ORGANIZATIONAL COMMUNICATION (PAGE 96)

Note that I have left the job titles capitalized in this letter, following the organization's house style. You might make them lower case or might at least query whether they should be lower case.

[Handwritten note in margin:] Note: I have changed Cogs Unlimited to CU after the first instance, per house style — ok?

To: All_Users
Subject: Introduction of Vice President, Operations
From: uni-mail@CU.com
Date: August 14, 2023

As President and CEO of Cogs Unlimited, it is my great pleasure to announce that our hiring committees search has been a success. Effective September 5, 2023, Alexa Sarnia, MBA will step into the role of Vice-President, Operations. As many of you will remember, Alexa was the Prairie Provinces Regional Manager from 2009 to 2015. Those of you with really long memories might know that Alexa started at the Cogs Unlimited location in Brandon, Manitoba, as counter staff back in 1993! *[handwritten: /cu /a]*

In the Regional Manager's role, Alexa set a sterling example in many ways. She demonstrated efficient management of financial resources, developed new administrative structures and processes, initiated a market expansion into the Northwest Territories, and mentored managers and staff in 37 stores across his territory. Alexa *[handwritten: / her]* exemplifies the kind of ingenuity and work ethic Cogs Unlimited seeks all senior *[handwritten: /cu /in]* employees. She hopes to inspire all CU employees to greater efficiencies and sales achievements.

I began this search in February 2023 with the assistance of C-Suite Management Consultants, who reached out through their international networks of executive partners to develope the broadest possible pool of candidates. Their outreach germinated more than 80 interested individuals. The hiring committee included *[handwritten: / generated]* managers from all regional offices, to ensure the incoming candidate would fit the *[handwritten: / ,]* CU culture. After developing a short list and conducting three rounds of interviews, we fund our new VP. I wish to acknowledge the members of the hiring committee who gave so generously of their time to make this hire happen.

Please join me in warmly welcoming Alexa back to Cogs Unlimited. I'm proud that *[handwritten: /cu]* she's part of our corporate family.

I.M. Grench
President and CEO
This account is not monitored for user replies.

EXERCISE: PROOFREADING A BIBLIOGRAPHY (PAGES 97–98)

Bibliography

Anderson-Dargatz, Gail. *Race Against Time.* Victoria: Orca Book Publishers, 2016.

Atwood, Margaret. *The Burgess Shale: The Canadian Writing Landscape of the 1960s.* Edmonton: University of Alberta Press, 2017.

Biel, Joe. A People's Guide to Publishing: Build a Successful, Sustainable, Meaningful Book Business from the Ground Up. Portland, OR: Microcosm Publishing, 2018. *[ital] [tr]*

Bowen, Gail. *Sleuth: On Writing Mysteries.* Regina: University of Regina Press, 2018.

Britt, Fanny. *Forever Truffle.* Toronto: Groundwood Books, 2022.

Bright, Robin. *Sometimes Reading Is Hard.* Markham, ON: Pembroke Publshers, 2021. *[tr]*

Burch, C. Beth. *Grammar for Writers.* Bloomington, IN: Archway Publishing, 2017.

Dewar, Elaine. *The Handover.* Windsor, ON: Biblioasis, 2017.

Epp, Roger. *We Are All Treaty People.* Edmonton: University of Alberta Press, 2098. *(? What is the correct date?)*

Germano, William. *On Revision: The Only Writing That Counts.* Chicago and London: The University of Chicago Press, 2021.

Grafton, Sue. *Y Is for Yesterday.* New York: G.P. Putnam's Sons, 2017. Green, John. *The Fault in Our Stars.* New York: Penguin Books, 2014. *[¶]*

Greenberg, Susan L. *Editors Talk about Editing.* New York: Peter Lang, 2015.

Harman, Eleanor, ed. *The Thesis and the Book: A Guide for First-Time Academic Authors,* 2nd ed. Toronto: University of Toronto Press, 2003.

Houston, Keith. *The Book: A Cover-to-Cover Exploration of the Most Powerful Object of Our Time.* New York: W.W. Norton & Company, 2016. *[/e]*

Irvine, Dean, and Smaro Kamboureli, eds. *Editing as Cultural Practice in Canada.* Waterloo, ON: Wilfrid Laurier University Press, 2016. *(? confirm this is not lower-case L)*

Johnston, Aviaq. *Those Who Run in the Sky.* Iqaluit, NU: Inhabit Media Inc., 2017.

Johnston, Wayne. *The Old Lost Land of Newfoundland: Family, Memory, Fiction, and Myth.* Edmonton: NeWest Press, 2009.

Juby, Susan. *The Fashion Committee.* Toronto: Penguin Teen, 2018.

King, Thomas. *The Inconvenient Indian: A Curious Account of Native People in North America.* Illustrated edition. Toronto: Doubleday Canada, 2017.

Koller, Katherine. *Art Lessons*. Winnipeg: Enfield and Wizenty, 2016.

Koupal, Nancy Tystad, ed. *Pioneer Girl Perspectives: Exploring Laura Ingalls Wilder*. Pierre, SD: South Dakota Historical Society Press, 2017.

Kowalski, William. *Epic Game*. Victoria: Orca Book Publishers, 2016.

(ital) Lemay, Shawna. "The Flower Can Always Be Changing." Windsor, ON: Palimpsest Press, 2018.

Leach, Sara. *Slug Days*. Toronto: Pajama Press, 2017.

(caps) Lorimer, Rowland. *Ultra Libris: Policy, technology, and the creative economy of book publishing in Canada*. Toronto: ECW Press, 2012.

Mayr, Suzette. *Dr. Edith Vane and the Hares of Crawley Hall*. Toronto: Coach House Books, 2017.

McCue, Duncan. *Decolonizing Journalism: A Guide to Reporting in Indigenous Communities*. Don Mills, ON: Oxford University Press, 2023.

McDonell, Terry. *The Accidental Life: An Editor's Notes on Writing and Writers*. New York: Knopf, 2016.

McLeod, Neal. *100 Days of Cree*. Regina: University of Regina Press, 2016.

Mount, Nick. *Arrival: The Story of CanLit*. Toronto: House of Anansi Press, 2017.

Ng, Celeste. *Little Fires Everywhere*. New York: Penguin, 2017.

(ital) Novik, Naomi. Uprooted. New York: Del Rey, 2016.

Peters, John Durham. *Speaking into the Air: A History of the Idea of Communication*. Chicago: University of Chicago Press, 2001.

Prescott, Tara. *Poetic Salvage: Reading Mina Loy*. Bucknell University Press, 2016. *(tr)*

Pullman, Philip. *The Book of Dust: La Belle Sauvage*. New York: Knopf Brooks for Young Readers, 2017.

Robinson, Eden. *The Sasquatch at Home: Traditional Protocols and Modern Storytelling*. Edmonton: University of Alberta, 2011. / Press

Scalzi, John. *Don't Live for You, Obituary*. Burton, MI: Subterranean Press, 2017.

Sileika, Antanas. *The Barefoot Bingo Caller*. Toronto: ECW Press, 2017.

Smart, Maya Payne. *Reading for Our Lives: A Literacy Action Plan from Birth to Six*. New York: Avery, 2022. *(tr)*

Solnit, Rebecca. *Men Explain Things to Me*. Chicago: Haymarket Books, 2015.

Steeves, Andrew. *Sixty over Twenty*. Kentville, NS: Gaspereau Press, 2017.

Sword, Helen. *Air & Light & Time & Space: How Successful Academics Write*. Cambridge, MA: Harvard University Press, 2017.

Thomspon, Cheryl, and Miranda Campbell, eds. *Creative Industries in Canada*. Toronto and Vancouver: Canadian Scholars, 2022. *(rom)*

Weiner, Jennifer: *Hungry Heart: Adventures in Life, Love, and Writing*. New York: Washington Square Press, 2017.

Wohlleben, Peter. *The Hidden Life If Trees*. Vancouver: Greystone Books, 2016.

Zevin, Gabrielle. *Young Jane Young*. Chapel Hill, NC: Algonquin Books, 2018.

EXERCISE: PROOFREADING A RESUMÉ (PAGE 99)

Alice P. Liddell
Seeking a position in communications and community engagement where I can share and enhance my award-winning creativity and analytical skills

AB/ 555 Rabbit Hole Road
Didsbury, ~~Alberta~~ T0M 0W0
(403) 780-5555
APL@freemail.ca

Queen of Hearts Baked Goods, Calgary, Alberta
Manager, Communications and Marketing

2/ **KEY ACCOMPLISHMENTS**
- Lead a fledging company to local and regional customer brand */1* recognition through creative, energetic communication strategies
- Recognized by the Baking Association of Canada with gold medal awards in 2014 and 2017 for Industrial Content Marketing

DUTIES
- Solely responsible for planning, implementing, and evaluating communications and branding strategies for an industrial bakery with clients across Western Canada *(lc)*
- Writing and editing content and responding to followers across multiple social media channels
- Writing and editing website content, including twice-weekly blog posts
- Writing copy and developing visual concepts for print collateral including signage, posters, catalogues, flyers, and mailers
- Handling news releases, maintaining an up-to-date media contact list, and handling information and interview requests from media
- Special event planning

Alberta Theatre and Stage Network
Communications and Marketing Coordinator

- Writing and editing website copy
- Writing and editing a biweekly digital newsletter for more than 900 recipients across western Canada (members and general pubic) */1*
- Writing and designing print and digital marketing materials to promote ATSN events and members shows */ '/*
- Preparing grant proposals for operational and project funding

Regina University College Press
Marketing Assistant

- ~~Wrote~~ website copy and maintaining title information on website */Writing*
- Developed media contacts database */ing*
- ~~Wrote or co-wrote~~ catalogue descriptions for forthcoming titles */Writing / co-writing*
- Assisted with event planning and author relationships */ing*

Education
Global Standard Certification (ongoing, */≠*
 International Association of Business
 Communicators Academy

BA (English Literature)
 Regina University College
High School Diploma (Honours)
 J.A. Fife High School, Olds */s AB*

References available upon request

EXERCISE: PROOFREADING A SOCIAL MEDIA TIMELINE (PAGES 100–101)

Ambrose Village

The riverside community that's anything but flat! Join our smart green development by the Saskatchewan River.

 Ambrose Village @AmbroseVillageYXE Sep 2

Happy Labour Day! Our Business Office is closed this weekend, but be sure to check out our newest show home on Cavanaugh Road. #showhome #VillageLiving

 Ambrose Village @AmbroseVillageYXE Aug 23

Its back to school next week. Looking for a welcoming community with a K–8 school your kids can walk to? Check out Seesequasis School at the heart of Ambrose Village. #families #schooldays #AutumnIsComing

 Ambrose Village @AmbroseVillageYXE Aug 13

It sure is hot! Don't forget your refillable water bottle. Wear a hat that shades your face. Keep kids and pets out of hot vehicles. Tomorrow's prediction: more of the same! #YXEWX #weather #hot

 Ambrose Village @AmbroseVillageYXE Aug 2

Looking for something to do this long weekend? Go for a stroll in beautiful Tomson Park at the centre of Ambrose Village. Follow Yurkiw Road from 1st Street. The kids will love our playground!

#families #play #summer

 Ambrose Village @AmbroseVillageYXE Jul 17

Guests visiting Saskatoon this summer? Keep them cool at the YWCA pool, just one block from the northeast corner of Ambrose Village. Check out a map here: tiny.url/4321 #swimming #summer #VillageLiving

 Ambrose Village @AmbroseVillageYXE Jul 8

Join CKXM Radio at our show homes on Bowen Blvd this Saturday, July 13, 1 to 4 pm. Giveaways, music, plus enter to win $10,000 dollars toward the purchase of you new home in Ambrose Village.

#prizes #showhome #VillageLiving

Ambrose Village @AmbroseVillageYXE Jul 1

Happy Canada Day, everyone! Join our street party on Bury Road between 1st and 4th. Face painting, snacks, family fun. Fireworks at 11:00 pm! #celebrate #Canada #summer

 Ambrose Village @AmbroseVillageYXE Jun 25

Until the end of July, you can save up to $28,000 on a new home in Ambrose Village Phase 5. Drop by one of our show homes or visit www.AmbroseVillageYXE.ca for more details.

 Ambrose Village @AmbroseVillageYXE Jun 18

Are you ready for The Saskatchewan Jazz Festival? Running June 22 to 29, it's a bonanza of music, musicians, and fun. Several of the venues are just steps form Ambrose Village. #jazz #music #FunIsHere

 Ambrose Village @AmbroseVillageYXE Jun 3

This is the month of the Strawberry Moon, according to Indigenous tradition. Maybe you should plant some strawberries in your new home garden! #VillageLiving #gardening #sweet

 Ambrose Village @AmbroseVillageYXE May 20

Happy Victoria Day! The business office is closed for the long weekend, but check our out show home parade along Cavanaugh Road. #showhome #VillageLiving #celebrate #summer

 Ambrose Village @AmbroseVillageYXE May 15

Just a reminder that with the spring weather, the streets around Tomson playground will be busier. Please watch your speed and keep our community safe! #kids #safety #VillageLiving

 Ambrose Village @AmbroseVillageYXE May 12

We wish mothers everywhere a cheerful and loving Mother's Day. And to our own moms, hello and thanks, with lots of love. #celebrate #moms

APPENDIX 1

Punctuation Primer

Punctuation explained

Here's a quick refresher for the basic marks of English punctuation. If you need more details or support, see appendix 5. Many people confuse the names of punctuation marks, so check that you and your writers mean the same thing when you communicate.

period: A period (or *full stop*) appears at the end of a DECLARATIVE SENTENCE: a sentence that makes a statement — that is, most sentences. (A question mark does the same job for an INTERROGATIVE SENTENCE — a direct question — and an exclamation point does it for an EXCLAMATION — an expression of intense feeling.) A period may also appear at the end of an abbreviation or after each letter of an acronym.

comma: The comma has many roles in sentences. Here are some big ones:

- Joining INDEPENDENT CLAUSES (complete sentences) with the help of a COORDINATING CONJUNCTION (*and, but, or, nor, yet, so, for*) (1)
- Separating elements in lists with (2a) or without (2b) a SERIAL COMMA
- Separating adjectives in series (in place of *and*) (3)
- Setting off non-essential and parenthetical sentence elements (commas often appear in pairs here) (4)
- Setting off initial sentence modifiers (before the SUBJECT of the sentence) (5)

Here are some examples demonstrating each of these comma functions:

(1) Arne loves cheese, <u>but</u> it's not good for his health.

(2a) Sarah needs to bring chocolate chips, olive oil, vanilla extract, <u>and</u> flour to class today.

(2b) Sarah needs to bring chocolate chips, olive oil, vanilla extract <u>and</u> flour to class today.

(3) Maribel made a <u>gentle, loving</u> gesture.

(4) Her first novel, *A Plague on Both Your Houses,* used unconventional narration. (Here an APPOSITIVE PHRASE is enclosed by paired commas. You could remove the phrase and the sentence would mean the same thing but would be missing a detail. Another take on the same content might enclose a clause instead: *Her first novel,* <u>which adopted unconventional narration,</u> *was titled* A Plague on Both Your Houses.)

(5) <u>After six days,</u> the itching diminished.

Commas may also be used stylistically to guide the reader or to shift emphasis within a sentence. These are rarely the problem commas, however.

semicolon: The major role of the semicolon is to join one independent clause to another independent clause without using a coordinating conjunction. There is normally a close topic relationship between the clauses (1). Semicolons may also be used alongside commas in complicated lists (2) and may be used to indicate coordination, or balance, in very long constructions (3). Here are some examples demonstrating these semicolon functions:

(1) Last summer we travelled to Bordeaux; there, we learned to enjoy claret.

(2) The tour took Amanda Palmer to Portland, Oregon; Vancouver, British Columbia; Edmonton, Alberta; and Billings, Montana.

(3) Gemma realized, after long reflection, that the appropriate response to Oscar's behaviour was icy politeness; but because of her accommodating nature, she continued to approach their meetings with good cheer and enthusiasm.

colon: A main role of the colon is similar to that of the semicolon: to join an independent clause to another independent clause without using a coordinating conjunction. When we connect sentences with a colon, however, the second clause explains, amplifies, or gives an example of the first clause (1). A colon can also introduce a word or phrase that explains, amplifies, or exemplifies the introductory clause (2a); in some kinds of writing, this function can include the introduction of direct quotations (2b). You may use a colon after the OBJECT of a verb to introduce a list (3a), but *don't* place a colon between a verb and its object (3b). Here are some examples:

(1) These beliefs are not entirely misplaced, either: they reflect the perceptions of graduate students of all ages, genders, and racialized identities.

(2a) Society at large communicates a bias against mental health: a bias that suggests mental illness is not simply an illness but a weakness.

(2b) In his letter to the board, Edouard Pelland pointed out the problem: "We argue that we're publishing books and authors in our local communities; the funders' argument against us is that

we're not writing or printing the books ourselves."

(3a) I placed my order for lunch: a chicken salad and side of soup. (Note that what precedes the colon is a full sentence; what follows is a detail about what was ordered.)

(3b)   (**wrong**) I ordered: a case of hair gel, three miniskirts, and new roller skates.

(**corrected**) I ordered a case of hair gel, three miniskirts, and new roller skates.

apostrophe: An apostrophe is used to indicate contraction (e.g., *won't*, *she's*, *they'd*) and possession. The use of apostrophes in contractions is fairly clear, but their use in possessives tends to be troublesome even for experienced writers. Any possessive (that is, any place where we express *the Y's X*) should be able to be read correctly as a phrase (*the X of the Y*), as in these examples:

My daughter's room = the room of my daughter

My daughters' room = the room of my daughters

hyphen: A hyphen is used to create a compound: a compound noun (1) or a compound modifier (2). It may be used in ADJECTIVE PHRASES that are PRENOMINAL (3) or, sometimes, PREDICATIVE (4). A hyphen may also indicate the break in a word at the end of a line (5). Here are some examples:

(1) The children were fascinated by the <u>fire-eater</u>.

(2) We painted our new barn <u>fire-engine</u> red.

(3) Dr. Ayling was a <u>well-loved</u> professor. (but *Professor Ayling was <u>well loved</u>.*)

(4) Kelly was looking for a full-time job. Now Kelly is working <u>full-time</u>.

(5) When I needed encouragement, my parents would remind me of the <u>little</u> engine that could.

dash: A dash — sometimes called a *double dash* or an *em dash* — is a mark that shows interruption or a break in the flow of a sentence (1). Dashes may also be used to set off a parenthetical construction that contains its own punctuation (2 and 3). Here are a few examples:

(1) As I was saying — wait, is that our car alarm?

(2) The prickly wild rose — *Rosa acicularis*, if you like the precision of a Latin name — was adopted as Alberta's provincial flower in 1930.

(3) Mortimer was grumpy again — he was always grumpy lately, wasn't he? — and Helena cringed inwardly at the probable trajectory of their morning together.

In typesetting, dashes may be SET WIDE or SET CLOSE. A dash set wide has a space before and after it, while a dash set close touches the adjacent letters — no space between the characters. This book uses dashes set wide.

The dash has one close relative, the en dash (–). Slightly longer than a hyphen and shorter than a dash, the en dash is used, among other things, to express ranges and, in some styles, relationships (in place of the word *to*), as in these examples:

mother–son bond

November–February term

1897–1977

pages 45–54

When you proofread, check hyphens, en dashes, and em dashes carefully: writers often use one where they want another. It's easy to distinguish between a hyphen and an em dash, but an en dash can fool even an experienced editor.

parentheses: Parentheses set off parts of sentences or sometimes complete sentences, including their terminal punctuation. They are always used in pairs.

Brackets, sometimes called *square brackets* or *editorial brackets*, are closely related to parentheses. They have two major functions in writing: to show editorial changes made to quoted text (1) and to nest a parenthetical within parentheses (2). Here is an example of each function:

(1) Josée notes that her findings "signal[led] a potential crisis brewing" in health sciences communications as early as 2008.

(2) But in a later edition of *What the Crow Said* (Kroetsch, 1998 [originally published 1978]), the spelling varies.

APPENDIX 2

Grammar Primer

Common grammar errors

Here's a quick refresher for some basic grammar errors. If you need more details or support, consult other resources such as those listed in appendix 5.

Remember that as a proofreader, you may have limited authority to change grammar unless the error is obvious, egregious, or likely to confuse readers. That means you may have to query some errors. See chapter 1 for guidance.

subject–verb agreement: The SUBJECT of a sentence must agree in NUMBER and PERSON with the main sentence verb. The basic rule is that a plural subject (including a COMPOUND SUBJECT joined with *and*) requires a plural verb (1a and 1b), and a singular subject (including a COLLECTIVE NOUN in most cases) requires a singular verb (2a and 2b).

(1a) Dance videos make fascinating viewing.

(1b) Both Ruth and Doug speak German.

(2a) Métis author Maria Campbell speaks four languages fluently.

(2b) A flock of chickens makes an unusual gift.

As in example 2b, be sure the verb agrees with the true subject (*a flock*), not a modifier or phrase between the subject and verb (*of chickens*). Watch out for verbs that occur before the subject (e.g., in a question). Here is an example:

(**wrong**) Have Esther or Janja ever been to the ballet before tonight?

(**corrected**) Has Esther or Janja ever been to the ballet before tonight?

Here are a few more points to watch:

- When a compound subject is created using *or* or *nor*, agreement is controlled by the subject element closer to the verb (e.g., *Neither the clinician nor the patients were happy with the test results* versus *Neither the patients nor the clinician was happy with the test results*).

- Some nouns appear to be plural in form but (usually) function as singular (e.g., *ethics, measles, mumps, news, statistics*).

- Some pronouns are controlled by their modifiers (particularly *any, some,* and *all,* as in *Some of this food is unappealing* versus *Some of these foods are unappealing*).

- The pronoun *none* may be understood to be plural or singular (and people tend to have strong feelings about the perspective they adopt, as in *None of these choices is suitable* versus *None of these choices are suitable*). Be consistent.

pronoun issues: A pronoun must have a clear and logical referent (or ANTECEDENT) with which it agrees in person, number, and sometimes GENDER. As with subject–verb agreement, the basic rule is that a singular antecedent requires a singular pronoun and a plural antecedent requires a plural pronoun. (The antecedent itself may be a pronoun.)

The most common pronoun-agreement issue occurs between *they* and indefinite pronouns that use *-one* or *-body* (e.g., *someone, anyone, everybody*). These pronouns are grammatically singular, while *they* is grammatically plural. Look at these examples (the verbs carry the clues):

> Everybody loves Raymond. They love Robert, too.

> Someone has left a jacket in the locker room. They have left their worries behind.

> Everyone needs to remember their key.

Some editors would change the third example to read *Everyone needs to remember his or her key*; but many wouldn't. The clash is between the strict logic of grammar and how a living language works — and English writers (and speakers) have been using *they/them/their* with singular antecedents for centuries.

At the copyediting stage, the solution to this clash may be to recast a sentence in the plural: *Everyone does better when he or she can make life choices freely* versus *People do better when they can make life choices freely* or *We all do better when we can make life choices freely*.

Using the plural form in English masks the gendered nature of our singular pronouns. Keep in mind two points. First, pronoun questions apply in the third person only — when the text is talking about someone (he/she/they/him/her/them). Second, if someone tells you which pronoun he/she/they would prefer, respect that request (many non-binary people prefer *they* rather than *he* or *she*, both of which are gendered and singular). The issue of using *they* rather than *he* or *she* (or *one*, if you're feeling high-handed) can be troubling, particularly in linguistically conservative situations, but by the time a text reaches the proofreader, the use of one pronoun set or another has usually been clearly established.

A RELATIVE PRONOUN (*that, which, who, whom,* or *whose*) must be replaceable by its referent word or phrase. Solve faulty or weak pronoun agreement by changing the pronoun or, if you have the authority, recasting the sentence.

One more thing. Be sure any personal pronouns reflect the correct grammatical case (the form of a word relative to its position in the sentence, such as *I* versus *me* or *she* versus *her*). A rough rule is that SUBJECT PRONOUNS are used before the sentence verb and OBJECT PRONOUNS are used in the predicate, but there are a few points to watch. For example,

> She and I will leave next Saturday. [subject of sentence]

> Stu's stories always gave us kids the shivers. [predicate of sentence]
> The medal was awarded to him. [object pronoun used as object of preposition]

> Your nemesis is I, your long-lost cousin! [subject pronoun used as subjective complement]

dangling modifier: A DANGLING MODIFIER occurs when a modifier has nothing to modify. Dangling modifiers are thus illogical and confusing, although sometimes funny. You can solve dangling modifiers in one of two ways: turn the modifier into a DEPENDENT CLAUSE (with a subject and a verb) or insert a logical word or phrase in the main clause for the modifier to modify. Here are some examples with solutions:

(**dangling modifier**) Having missed the train, a long wait now seemed unavoidable.

(**correction option 1**) Because we had missed the train, a long wait now seemed unavoidable.

(**correction option 2**) Having missed the train, we now faced a long wait.

(**dangling modifier**) Undeterred by criticism, publication was Brady's goal.

(**correction option 1**) As Brady was undeterred by criticism, publication was his goal.

(**correction option 2**) Undeterred by criticism, Brady sought publication.

misplaced modifier: A MISPLACED MODIFIER occurs when a modifier is too far from what it modifies to form a clear, logical relationship. You solve the issue by moving the modifier close to the word or phrase it modifies; there is often more than one way to solve a misplaced modifier, so use the context of the sentence to guide you. Here are some examples with solutions:

(**misplaced modifier**) The boy gazed at the puppy snuffling along the boulevard <u>longingly</u>.

(**corrected**) The boy gazed longingly at the puppy snuffling along the boulevard.

(**misplaced modifier**) The writer promised <u>before Canada Day</u> to return the manuscript.

(**correction option 1**) The writer promised to return the manuscript before Canada Day.

(**correction option 2**) Before Canada Day, the writer promised to return the manuscript.

comma splice: A COMMA SPLICE is created when two complete sentences are joined with only a comma and without a conjunction or other punctuation. Comma splices are extremely common, but commonness doesn't make them correct; they are better accepted in fiction and creative nonfiction than in technical or academic prose. A comma splice may be solved in one of three ways:

1. Separate the two sentences with a period.
2. Replace the comma with a semicolon (or in some cases, a colon).

3. Insert a coordinating conjunction (*and, but, or, nor, yet, so, for*) after the comma (when the sentence can logically accept one), or insert a SUBORDINATING CONJUNCTION (e.g., *although, because, if, since, unless, until, whereas, while*) and omit the comma.

Here is an example with solutions:

(**comma splice**) Plant conifers on the west side of your house, they provide shade in the summer and shelter from the wind in the winter.

(**correction option 1**) Plant conifers on the west side of your house. They provide shade in the summer and shelter from the wind in the winter.

(**correction option 2**) Plant conifers on the west side of your house; they provide shade in the summer and shelter from the wind in the winter.

(**correction option 3**) Plant conifers on the west side of your house because they provide shade in the summer and shelter from the wind in the winter.

Be sure your solution suits your intended audience: some people *really* dislike semicolons!

run-together sentence: A RUN-TOGETHER SENTENCE (also known as a *fused sentence* or, more commonly, a *run-on sentence*) occurs when two or more complete sentences are joined without punctuation or conjunctions. Run-together sentences may be solved the way comma splices are: by separating the sentences with a period, separating the sentences with a semicolon, or inserting an appropriate conjunction between the sentences. Here is an example with solutions:

(**run-together sentence**) My close friend
        once played in the NHL he
        now teaches high school math.
(**correction option 1**) My close friend
        once played in the NHL. He
        now teaches high school math.
(**correction option 2**) My close friend
        once played in the NHL; he
        now teaches high school math.
(**correction option 3**) My close friend
        once played in the NHL, but
        he now teaches high school
        math.

Be sure not to create a comma splice when you
resolve a run-together sentence. Also be aware
that run-together sentences are very common
on social media (e.g., the popular construction "I'm not crying you're crying," also seen
as "I'm not crying, you're crying") and may be
used intentionally there.

sentence fragment: A sentence fragment is a
group of words that expresses an incomplete
thought. It lacks a subject, a main verb, or
both a subject and a main verb. Fragments are
common in creative writing but uncommon
in technical or formal prose such as annual
reports, policy documents, and news releases.
To resolve a fragment, insert the missing
sentence component or components. In general, when you're proofreading, correct only
uncontrolled fragments; let stylistic fragments
stand. Here are some examples:

(**uncontrolled**) We found our lost puppy.
        Huddling under a shrub
        and trying to stay out of the
        rain. When she recognized
        Ezra, she bounded toward us
        instantly.
(**corrected**) We found our lost puppy
        huddling under a shrub
        and trying to stay out of the
        rain. When she recognized

Ezra, she bounded toward us
        instantly.
(**stylistic**) O waste of loss, in the hot
        mazes, lost, among bright stars
        on this most weary unbright
        cinder, lost! Remembering
        speechlessly we seek the
        great forgotten language, the
        lost lane-end into heaven, a
        stone, a leaf, an unfound door.
        Where? When? (from Thomas
        Wolfe, *Look Homeward, Angel*)

parallelism: PARALLELISM (also known as
parallel structure) is based on balance. It leans
on repetition to make phrasing memorable
and elegant but requires a close review to
ensure no items are omitted or unnecessarily
repeated. Here's an example:

(**not parallel**) This monument celebrates
        those who have, are currently,
        or will teach in the future.
(**corrected**) This monument celebrates
        those who have taught, are
        currently teaching, or will
        teach in the future.

To solve parallelism problems, ensure that
each element is grammatically balanced and
flows smoothly from its lead-in, repeating or
omitting modifiers and determiners as necessary. Here's another example:

(**not parallel**) I feel strongly — as an
        Albertan, a Canadian, and as
        a citizen of the world — that
        we must do more to draw
        attention to the plight of the
        woodland caribou.
(**correction option 1**) I feel strongly — as
        an Albertan, as a Canadian,
        and as a citizen of the world —
        that we must do more to draw
        attention to the plight of the
        woodland caribou.

(**correction option 2**) I feel strongly — as an Albertan, a Canadian, and a citizen of the world — that we must do more to draw attention to the plight of the woodland caribou.

active and passive voice: In active voice, the subject performs the main sentence verb. In passive voice, the verb is enacted by the subject. In general, writing in the active voice is briefer, clearer, and more interesting, but there is always a place for the passive voice, particularly when our focus is on outcomes and consequences.

(**active**) N.K. Jemisin won the Hugo Award in 2018.

(**passive**) The Hugo Award was won by N.K. Jemisin in 2018.

(**active**) Women pilots ferried Spitfires and Hurricanes between England and France during World War Two.

(**passive**) Spitfires and Hurricanes were ferried between England and France by women pilots during World War Two.

The subject of the active sentence shifts into a prepositional phrase (called an *agent phrase*) in the passive voice and can be omitted from the sentence. Agent phrases are often omitted to shift focus from actor to outcome.

(**active**) Our staff makes fresh bread daily in our bakery.

(**passive**) Fresh bread is made daily in our bakery ~~by us~~.

(**active**) The evaluators sorted the dogs by size and sex.

(**passive**) The dogs were sorted by size and sex ~~by the evaluators~~.

Sometimes, omitting the agent phrase removes an important idea from the sentence (e.g., in my first group of examples, removing the agent phrase "by women pilots" obscures an important historical fact). Thus, there may be an ethical consideration to using the passive voice, and communicators in sensitive settings sometimes lean hard on the ambiguity, for example, *Mistakes were made* (by whom?) or *Funds were misappropriated* (by whom?). When you're proofreading, the major concern is whether the absence of the grammatical actor may cause confusion for the audience; if that's the case, you may have to recast the sentence.

Writers can easily create dangling modifiers in passive voice because the passive removes the subject of the modifier; but unless the dangling modifier is laugh-out-loud silly, at this stage, don't rewrite the sentence.

(**dangling**) Having pursued the allegations, ample evidence of election fraud was discovered.

(**corrected**) Having pursued the allegations, investigators discovered ample evidence of election fraud.

(**dangling**) To support our fundraising goals, a bake sale will be held.

(**correction option 1**) To support our fundraising goals, we will hold a bake sale.

(**correction option 2**) We will hold a bake sale to support our fundraising goals.

APPENDIX 3

Some Troublesome Words and Phrases

A basic principle in thinking like a proofreader involves anticipating where errors may occur. One common problem that proofreaders encounter involves words and phrases that may have been misheard or miskeyed or that are uncommon and therefore frequently misspelled. The list below is meant to get you thinking about where trouble might occur when you're proofreading. While by no means exhaustive, this list captures errors that I have seen often. I hope you will add your own examples as your proofreading experience grows.

amount (versus *number*: *amount* is used with things that are indivisible [e.g., "a large amount of wine"]; *number* is used with things that are divisible and countable [e.g., "a large number of people"])

argument

assess (may be miskeyed as *asses*, and vice versa)

begin (may be miskeyed as *being*, and vice versa)

beginner, beginning

boulevard

cachet (pronounced *ca-shay*; often misspelled as *cache*)

casual (may be miskeyed as *causal*, and vice versa)

clothes (may be miskeyed as *cloths*, and vice versa)

course (may be miskeyed as *source*, and vice versa)

created (may be miskeyed as *crested*, and vice versa)

definite, definitely

diary (may be miskeyed as *dairy*, and vice versa)

each other's (the apostrophe is often misplaced)

environment

except (may be miskeyed as *expect*, and vice versa; may be heard as a homophone for *accept*)

forty

gateway (may be miskeyed as *getaway*, and vice versa)

government

grammar

maintenance

mature (may be miskeyed as *nature*, and vice versa)

mediation (may be miskeyed as *meditation*, and vice versa)

outage (may be miskeyed as *outrage*, and vice versa)

peace of mind (may be confused with the phrase *piece of [one's] mind*)

precious (may be miskeyed as *previous*, and vice versa)

promoted (may be miskeyed as *prompted*, and vice versa)

public (may be miskeyed as *pubic*; scan for this error using search/replace tools) segue (often misspelled as *segway*)

spilt (may be miskeyed as *split*, and
vice versa)

subpoena

supersede

trial (may be miskeyed as *trail*, and
vice versa)

undeserved (may be miskeyed as
underserved, and vice versa)

uniformed (may be miskeyed as
uninformed, and vice versa)

violent (may be miskeyed as *violet*,
and vice versa)

weird

whoa (not *woah*)

Commonly Confused Words

Another common problem proofreaders encounter is confused diction (the use of one word in place of another for any number of reasons). The list below provides a healthy selection of words that are frequently confused, and it may help you anticipate these and other diction issues. Once you start thinking about these issues, you'll find similar lists online and in books about diction, usage, and editing (including some of the texts listed in appendix 5).

a lot	allot			choose	chose	
accept	except			chord	cord	
ad	add			cite	sight	site
adapt	adopt			climactic	climatic	
addition	edition			coma	comma	
adverse	averse			complement	compliment	
advice	advise			conscience	conscious	
affect	effect			council	counsel	consul (also console)
aisle	isle			decent	descent	
all ready	already			defuse	diffuse	
all together	altogether			dependant	dependent	
allude	elude			desert	dessert	
allusion	illusion			discreet	discrete	
altar	alter			disinterested	uninterested	
amoral	immoral			dual	duel	
ascent	assent			dyeing	dying	
bare	bear			elicit	illicit	
bated	baited			enormity	enormousness	
berth	birth			envelop	envelope	
born	borne			every day	everyday	
brake	break			faze	phase	
breach	breech			flair	flare	
bread	bred			flaunt	flout	
breath	breathe			foreword	forward	
canvas	canvass			full	fulsome	
cent	scent	sent				

gorilla	guerilla		pole	poll	
hear	here		pore	pour	
hoard	horde		precede	proceed	
install	instill		prescribed	proscribed	
it's	its		principal	principle	
lay (laid)	lie (lain)		rack	wrack	
lead	led		rain	reign	rein
lessen	lesson		restful	restive	
let's	lets		ring	wring	
lightening	lightning		role	roll	
loath	loathe		sew	sow	so
loose	lose		sight	site	cite
lustful	lusty		stationary	stationery	
mantel	mantle		tail	tale	
medal	meddle		than	then	
metal	mettle		their	there	they're
moot	mute		to	too	two
noisome	noisy		valance	valence	
pain	pane		waist	waste	
pair	pare		waive	wave	
palate	palette	pallet	we're	were	where
passed	past		weather	whether	
peer	pier		who	whom	
personal	personnel		who's	whose	
plain	plane		you're	your	

APPENDIX 5

Selected Resources

WRITING AND COMPOSITION

William Strunk, Jr. and E.B. White, *The Elements of Style*, 4th ed. (Boston: Allyn and Bacon, 2000).

Joseph M. Williams, *Style: Ten Lessons in Clarity and Grace*, 6th ed. (New York: Longman, 2000).

William Zinsser, *On Writing Well*, 30th Anniversary ed. (New York: HarperCollins, 2006).

GRAMMAR AND PUNCTUATION

Bas Aarts, *Oxford Modern English Grammar* (Oxford: Oxford University Press, 2011).

Karen Elizabeth Gordon, *The Deluxe Transitive Vampire* (New York: Pantheon Books, 1993).

Karen Elizabeth Gordon, *The New Well-Tempered Sentence* (New York: Mariner Books, 2001).

Patricia T. O'Conner, *Woe Is I*, updated and expanded 4th ed. (New York: Riverhead Books, 2019).

Bruce Ross-Larson, *Edit Yourself* (New York: W.W. Norton & Company, 1996).

Maxine Ruvinsky, *Practical Grammar*, 3rd ed. (Don Mills, ON: Oxford University Press, 2014).

DICTION AND USAGE

Katherine Barber, ed., *Canadian Oxford Dictionary*, 2nd ed. (Don Mills, ON: Oxford University Press, 2004).

Bill Bryson, *Troublesome Words*, 3rd ed. (London: Penguin Books, 2001).

Benjamin Dreyer, *Dreyer's English: An Utterly Correct Guide to Clarity and Style* (New York: Random House, 2019).

Ann Ehrlich et al., *Medical Terminology for Health Professions*, 9th ed. (Boston: Cengage Learning, 2021).

Margery Fee and Janice McAlpine, *Guide to Canadian English Usage*, 2nd ed. (Don Mills, ON: Oxford University Press, 2011).

McGraw-Hill Dictionary of Scientific and Technical Terms, 6th ed. (New York: McGraw-Hill, 2003).

Bill Walsh, *The Elephants of Style* (New York: McGraw-Hill, 2004).

Bill Walsh, *Lapsing into a Comma* (Lincolnwood, IL: Contemporary Books, 2000).

STYLE GUIDES

The Chicago Manual of Style, 17th ed. (Chicago: University of Chicago Press, 2017).

Council of Science Editors, *Scientific Style and Format*, 8th ed. (Chicago: University of Chicago Press, 2014).

Editing Canadian English, 3rd ed. (Toronto: Editors' Association of Canada, 2015).

James McCarten, ed., *The Canadian Press Stylebook*, 19th ed. (Toronto: The Canadian Press, 2021).

McGill Law Journal, *Canadian Guide to Uniform Legal Citation*, 10th ed. (Toronto: Carswell, 2023).

William A. Sabin et al., *The Gregg Reference Manual*, 10th Canadian ed. (N.p.: McGraw-Hill Education, 2022).

Gregory Younging, *Elements of Indigenous Style: A Guide for Writing By and About Indigenous Peoples* (Edmonton: Brush Education, 2018).

EDITORIAL TRAINING

Editors Canada (editors.ca) offers a variety of webinars, many of which are available for viewing on YouTube.

The Indigenous Editors Association (indigenouseditorsassociation.com) supports Indigenous editors and others in publishing and communications by sharing knowledge and practices rooted in Indigenous knowledge and epistemology.

Louise Harnby offers training courses for editors and writers, emphasizing professionalism and efficiency. https://www.louiseharnbyproofreader.com/courses.html.

Adrienne Montgomerie offers online training in many areas, including how to mark up PDF documents. https://www.scieditor.ca.

Carol Fisher Saller's delightful book *The Subversive Copy Editor* (2nd ed. 2016) puts proofreading and copyediting into a broader context of editorial judgement and practical application.

Glossary

adjective phrase: a single word or a phrase that describes a noun or noun-like word or phrase

antecedent: the noun (or noun-like structure) that a pronoun refers to; the pronoun and antecedent must agree in number, person, and gender

appositive phrase: a phrase that gives additional information about a subject or an object in a sentence

auxiliary: a word that supports the main sentence verb; may be a form of *to be, to have,* or *to do* or a modal auxiliary (*can, could, shall, should, will, would, may, might, must*)

bad break: line-end hyphenation that interrupts smooth reading and tidy mechanics, such as hyphenating a proper noun, hyphenating a word in the middle of a syllable, or hyphenating an already hyphenated word

boilerplate copy: generic copy that can be made specific by adding details (e.g., a contract or a form letter)

catch: an error a proofreader has found

collective noun: a noun that expresses a group or collection of things (e.g., a flock, a herd, a pack); normally understood to be grammatically singular

comma splice: a grammar error created when two complete sentences are joined with only a comma

comparison proofreading: the process in which the current copy of a document (the "live" copy) is checked against the previous version of that document (the "dead" copy)

compound subject: a noun joined to one or more other nouns, together forming the subject of a sentence (e.g., *Unicorns, narwhals, and winged horses share some common features*)

consolidating changes: the process of reviewing multiple proofreaders' catches and assembling them into a single document so there exists only one master version of the "live" proof

coordinating conjunction: one of seven words that join single words, phrases, or clauses to create balanced constructions: *and, but, or, nor, yet, so, for*

dangling modifier: a modifying phrase or clause that lacks a logical element in the sentence to modify; considered a grammar error

declarative sentence: a sentence that makes a statement (e.g., *We saw you waving at us*)

dependent clause: a clause introduced by a subordinating conjunction, relative pronoun, complementizer, relative adverb, or interrogative; the clause can't stand alone as a sentence (e.g., *When we last met*)

digital printing: the process of printing directly from a digital document without the use of a printing plate

display type: eye-catching type used in short segments of text such as headlines, posters, advertisements, and book covers

editorial triage: a process of decision making that evaluates the most urgent needs in a text and deals with them as a priority

exclamation: a statement expressed with strong feeling or immediacy (e.g., *It's so fluffy, I'm going to die!*); may be a phrase or a complete sentence; indicated by an exclamation point

FPO: "for position only"; an abbreviation that identifies content that will be replaced before publication

gender: marker that signals whether a pronoun refers to a male antecedent, a female antecedent, or an ungendered antecedent

independent clause: a group of words that includes a subject and a predicate and that makes a complete statement: a complete sentence

interrogative sentence: a sentence that asks a direct question (e.g., *Do you hear that strange sound?*); indicated by a question mark

justification: aligning type to both right and left margins to create a smooth, even shape on the page

loose lines: lines of type visually marred by uneven, wide word spacing

mechanics: conventions regarding the treatment of written text, such as the use of underlining versus italics, how numbers are represented (as words or as numerals), and when words are capitalized

misplaced modifier: a modifying word, phrase, or clause that appears too far from the sentence element it modifies to form a clear, logical relationship; considered a grammar error

number: marker that signals whether a word is singular or plural

object (of a verb): a noun or pronoun on which a sentence verb acts; may be direct or indirect

object pronoun: a pronoun that receives the action of a verb or acts as the object of a preposition

offset printing: conventional printing technique in which ink from a printing plate is trans-ferred to the printing surface (usually but not always paper) using a rubber blanket

open compound: a phrase that is understood as a single idea or entity (e.g., *food stamp, side dish, milk run*)

parallelism (aka *parallel structure*): the use of grammatically similar structures to make language more appealing or more memorable; used for inline and vertical lists

pass: a complete read-through of a text or a partic-ular element of a text (e.g., all the captions, all the footers)

person: marker that signals whether an utterance refers to the speaker (first person), the listener/reader (second person), or the subject spoken about (third person)

predicative: a word or phrase that occurs in the predicate of a clause — as the object or a com-plement, for example

prenominal: appearing before a noun

recto: the right-hand side of a two-page spread; more broadly, the front side of a sheet of paper

relative pronoun: a pronoun used to introduce an adjectival clause (often called a *relative clause*): *that, which, who, whom, whose*

rivers (in text): gaps of white space within lines of type that emerge when there are multiple loose lines on the page

roman (type): type without bold or italic formatting

run-together sentence: construction created when two or more complete sentences are joined without punctuation or conjunctions

serial comma (aka *series comma* or *Oxford comma*): the comma that immediately precedes the coordinating conjunction (typically *and, but,* or *or*) in a list

set close: a dash with no space before or after it

set wide: a dash with a space before and after it

small caps: characters that resemble upper case letters but have a height and weight closer to lower case letters.

soft proofing: proofreading a document onscreen rather than on paper

stacked hyphens: the appearance of a hyphen at the end of three or more consecutive lines of type

standing copy: finished copy that may be repeat-edly repurposed verbatim (e.g., an organiza-tion's vision statement and goals or a publisher's description of a long-running series)

stet: let it stand; that is, do not make the change marked

style sheet: a project-specific record of decisions applied to a document (e.g., spellings, mechan-ical choices, and unusual proper names)

subject (of a sentence): a noun or pronoun that performs the action of the sentence

subject pronoun: a pronoun that stands in place of a noun as the subject (agent) of a sentence

subordinating conjunction: a word that joins clauses to create unbalanced or subordinate relationships within a sentence (e.g., *although, because, if, since, unless, until, whereas, while*)

substrate: a surface to which print is applied, e.g., paper or cardboard

TK: "to come": an abbreviation that identifies content that is not yet in place

verso: the left-hand page of a two-page spread; more broadly, the back side of a sheet of paper

vertical list: (aka *bulleted list*): content presented in display format, usually using parallel struc-ture to organize the content and bullets to separate the listed items

Bibliography

Alley, Michael. *The Craft of Editing: A Guide for Managers, Scientists, and Engineers.* New York: Springer, 2000.

Anderson, Laura. *McGraw-Hill's Proofreading Handbook.* 2nd ed. New York: McGraw-Hill, 2006.

Bernstein, Theodore M. *Miss Thistlebottom's Hobgoblins: The Careful Writer's Guide to the Taboos, Bugbears and Outmoded Rules of English Usage.* New York: The Noonday Press, 1991.

Bigwood, Sally, and Melissa Spore. *Presenting Numbers, Tables, and Charts.* Oxford: Oxford University Press, 2003.

Billingham, Jo. *Editing and Revising Text.* Oxford: Oxford University Press, 2002.

Butcher, Judith, Caroline Drake, and Maureen Leach. *Butcher's Copy-Editing: The Cambridge Handbook for Editors, Copy-Editors and Proofreaders.* 4th ed. Cambridge: Cambridge University Press, 2006.

Butler, Eugenia, Mary Ann Hickman, Patricia J. McAlexander, and Lalla Overby. *Correct Writing.* 6th ed. Lexington, MA: D.C. Heath and Company, 1995.

The Chicago Manual of Style. 17th ed. Chicago: University of Chicago Press, 2017.

Cummings, William. "White House Celebrates Economic Growth of the 'United Sates' in Twitter Typo." *USA Today*, 27 July 2018. https://www.usatoday.com/story/news/politics/onpolitics/2018/07/27/white-house-typo-united-sates/851907002/.

Davies, Ruth. "Atomic Typo — Yes, That's Really a Thing." *Ruth Davies: centrEditing*, 23 March 2013. https://centrediting.com.au/2013/03/23/atomic-typo-yes-thats-really-a-thing/.

"Did We Change the Definition of 'Literally'?" *Merriam-Webster.* https://www.merriam-webster.com/words-at-play/misuse-of-literally. Accessed 22 August 2018.

Dunham, Steve. *The Editor's Companion.* Cincinnati: Writer's Digest Books, 2014.

Editing Canadian English. 3rd ed. Toronto: Editors' Association of Canada, 2015.

Einsohn, Amy, and Marilyn Schwartz. *The Copyeditor's Handbook.* 4th ed. Berkeley: University of California Press, 2019.

Enos, Marcella F. "Instructional Interventions for Improving Proofreading and Editing Skills of College Students." *Business Communication Quarterly* 73.3 (September 2010): 265–81. https://doi.org/10.1177/1080569910376535.

Ginna, Peter, ed. *What Editors Do: The Art, Craft, and Business of Book Editing.* Chicago: University of Chicago Press, 2017.

Harnby, Louise. "Start-up Skills: Proofread Like It's 1976." *The Editing Blog*, 9 April 2016. https://www.louiseharnbyproofreader.com/blog/proofread-like-its-1976.

Henry, Jeanne. *The 11th Hour Edit.* Ann Arbor, MI: Promotional Perspectives, 1995.

Hill, Gerard M-F. *Punctuation: A Guide for Editors and Proofreaders.* London: Chartered Institute of Editing and Proofreading, 2021.

Hughes, Graham. *Editing and Proofreading Numbers*. London: Chartered Institute of Editing and Proofreading, 2021.

Hunter, Margaret. *Proofreading or Editing? A Quick Guide to Using Editorial Professionals*. London: Chartered Institute of Editing and Proofreading, 2020.

Ide, Kathy. *Polishing the "PUGS": Punctuation, Usage, Grammar, and Spelling Tips for Writers*. Enumclaw, WA: UpWrite Press, 2007.

Jenkins Townson, Nora (@NoraJKS). "OK but this is reindeer moss." 10 July 2019, 3:55 p.m. Tweet.

Komando, Kim. "How to Keep iPhone's Autocorrect in Check." *USA Today*, 21 April 2017. https://www.usatoday.com/story/tech/columnist/komando/2017/04/21/how-take-control-ios-iphone-autocorrect/100701986/.

Kristensson, Per Ola. "Do You Use Predictive Text? Chances Are It's Not Saving You Time — and Could Even Be Slowing You Down." *The Conversation*, 23 November 2021. https://theconversation.com/do-you-use-predictive-text-chances-are-its-not-saving-you-time-and-could-even-be-slowing-you-down-170163.

Lee, Marshall. *Bookmaking: Editing/Design/Production*. 3rd ed. New York: W.W. Norton & Company, 2004.

Malady, Matthew J.X. "Is It Time to Kill Autocorrect?" *Slate*, 1 July 2014. http://www.slate.com/articles/life/the_good_word/2014/07/autocorrect_fails_how_and_why_to_turn_off_word_prediction_on_your_phone.html.

May, Debra. *Proofreading Plain and Simple*. Clifton Park, NY: Delmar Cengage Learning, 2000.

Nichols, Wendalyn. "When You're on Deadline: Editorial Triage." Copyediting Audio Conference, 19 May 2009.

Norstrom, Barbara, and Mary Vines Cole. *Proofreading at the Computer*. 2nd ed. Mason, OH: Thomson South-Western, 2006.

Orr, Dona, Carol W. Henson, and H. Frances Daniels. *Proofreading: A Programmed Approach*. Mason, OH: South-Western / Thomson Learning, 2003.

Pagel, Larry G., and Barbara Norstrom. *Proofreading and Editing Precision*. 6th ed. Mason, OH: South-Western Cengage Learning, 2011.

Pavlovitz, John (@johnpavlovitz). "You do, huh?" 7 September 2018, 7:34 a.m. Tweet.

Perelman, Leslie C., James Paradis, and Edward Barrett. *The Mayfield Handbook of Technical and Scientific Writing*. Mountain View, CA: Mayfield Publishing Company, 1998.

Person, Tom. "The Burden of Proof." *Laughing Bear Newsletter*, April 1995. http://www.laughingbear.com/printable.asp?subMode=sp_burden.

Professional Editorial Standards. Toronto: Editors' Association of Canada, 2016.

Rosenkrantz, Otte. *Right Your Wrongs: Editorial Comments, Corrections and Guidelines*. Toronto: Thomson Nelson, 2006.

Rude, Carolyn D. *Technical Editing*. 3rd ed. New York: Longman, 2002.

Scott, Tom. "why typing like this is sometimes okay." YouTube video, 15 July 2019. https://youtu.be/fS4X1JfX6_Q.

Smith, Debra A., and Helen R. Sutton. *Powerful Proofreading Skills: Tips, Techniques and Tactics*. Menlo Park, CA: Crisp Publications, 1994.

Smith, Lynette M. *80 Common Layout Errors to Flag When Proofreading Book Interiors*. Yorba Linda, CA: All My Best, 2015.

Stet Again: More Tricks of the Trade for Publications People. Alexandria, VA: EEI Press, 1996.

Stevens, Helen, and Laura Ripper. "Proofreading Tip — Checking for Mistyped Words." *School Proof,* 20 April 2018. https://school-proof.weebly.com/blog/proofreading-tip-checking-for-mistyped-words.

Thaler-Carter, Ruth E. "Exploring the Editor's Task." *Copyediting* (April–May 2012) 1–3.

Tunney, Catharine. "The Glitch List: Ottawa to Start Reporting on Typos in Legislation." *CBC News,* 14 August 2018. https://www.cbc.ca/news/politics/justice-department-typo-letter-1.4784591.

Vanstone, Kay. *Practical Proofreading.* 2nd ed. Toronto: Copp Clark Ltd., 1997.

Williams, Allison K. *Seven Drafts: Self-Edit like a Pro from Blank Page to Book.* Norwalk, CT: Woodhall Press, 2021.

Yon, Daniel. "Now You See It." *Aeon.* 4 July 2019. https://aeon.co/essays/how-our-brain-sculpts-experience-in-line-with-our-expectations.

Younging, Gregory. *Elements of Indigenous Style: A Guide for Writing By and About Indigenous Peoples.* Edmonton: Brush Education, 2018.

Index

abbreviations, 33, 41, 43–44, 46; and autocorrection, 61; of editorial terms, 75, 153, 154; and periods, 80, 137; on style sheets, 8

acronyms, 43–44, 46; and autocorrection, 61; and periods, 137; on style sheets, 8

Adobe Acrobat, 7, 11

agent phrase, 145

agreement: pronoun–antecedent, 141–142; subject–verb, 49–51, 54, 55, 80, 83, 141

Alley, Michael, 6

antecedent, 54, 141, 142, 153

apostrophes, 35, 138; for contractions, 138; for possession, 37, 46, 54, 111, 138; vs. quotation marks, 38, 83

audience: editing for, 2, 3; and diction, 54; and grammar, 51–52, 143, 145; and informal language, 53—54; proofreading for, 2, 5, 19, 34; punctuation and, 36, 37, 46; queries informed by, 8; and reception of text, 2; relationship with, 29, 63; resources to suit, 10, 26. See also readers.

authority (of proofreader), 4, 5; and commas, 11; vs. of copyeditor, xiii; and copy-fitting, 75; and diction, 54; and grammar, 51, 141, 142; and parallelism, 44; and visual presentation, 74

autocompletion, 60–61, 64

autocorrection, 23, 29, 59, 60, 64

auxiliary (verbs), 59, 153

bad break, 36, 83, 153

Bernstein, Theodore M., 54

boilerplate copy, 80, 153

boundaries, 2, 4–6, 8, 66

brackets, 37, 139

capitalization, 33, 35, 38, 41–43; in Indigenous style, 41

captions, 6, 65, 69, 74, 86

catches, 4, 153; in proofreading process, 6, 30, 85; on style sheets, 24; and version management, 7, 79, 153

clarity, xi, 2, 51; of abbreviations and acronyms, 43; and commas, 34; vs. consistency, 33; of markup, 11

coherence, 2, 6

colons, 35, 37, 46, 83, 138, 143

comma, 34–35, 137; as confused word, 149; consistent use of, 46, 83; and introductory phrases, 33, 54; parenthetical, 34, 37, 137; and quotation marks, 38; and semicolons, 137; splice, 34, 143–144, 153; stray, 34; stylistic, 137. See also serial comma.

commitment to quality, xi, 4, 29, 84, 86

comparison proofreading, 61, 79, 153

compound: closed, 36, 106, 138; open, 25, 154; prenominal, 36, 138

compound subject, 55, 83, 141, 153

concentration, xii, 18, 86

conjunctions, 34, 41, 143; coordinating, 137, 138, 143, 153, 154; subordinating, 143, 153, 154

consistency: of abbreviations and acronyms, 43–44; of boilerplate copy, 80; vs. clarity, 33; in copyediting, 2, 3; vs. correctness, 6; of errors, 51, 61; of grammar, 51, 141; of late additions, 83, 86; of mechanics, 41, 43, 44, 76; of markup, 11, 18; as proofreader's role, xi, xii, 1, 3, 6, 57, 60, 83, 85; of punctuation, 34, 35, 36, 37, 46, 76; of spelling, 8, 24, 28, 30, 106; and style sheets and guides, 8–11, 37, 41; of treatment of numbers and data, 43, 64, 65, 66; of visual communication, 69–70, 75, 76, 86. See also inconsistency.

consolidating changes, 7, 86, 153

context: and autocorrection, 61; and errors in text, 63; of numbers and data, 64–65; proofreading in, xiv, 54; of text, xiii, 4; and vertical lists, 44; and visual presentation of text, 70; of words, xi, 10, 59, 60; and word choice, 64

copyediting: and dictionaries, 26; vs. proofreading, xii, xiii, 2, 18, 80, 83; in publishing sequence, 3, 49, 142

copyeditor: decisions made by, 43, 44; vs. proofreader, 1, 2, 18; and style sheets, 3, 9

copy-fitting, 75

correctness, 53–54; in copyediting, 2, 3; vs. consistency, 6; of late additions, 86; of mechanics, 43, 44; of numbers and data, 64, 65; as proofreader's role, xi, 1, 3, 5–6, 85; of punctuation 34, 35; vs. style, 29; and text-generation tools, 60, 61; of visual communication, 69–70, 74, 76

About the Author

Writer, editor, and professor Leslie Vermeer has worked in book publishing for more than twenty years, having edited or contributed to more than two hundred books to date. Leslie teaches at MacEwan University in Edmonton, Alberta, where her focus includes editing, grammar, and print culture studies. She is the author of *The Complete Canadian Book Editor* (2016), a comprehensive look at what book editors do.

For information about Leslie's current projects, check out ReadingWithAPencil.com.